KINGS & CHRONICLES

A HISTORY OF DIVIDED MONARCHY

Greg A. King

Pacific Press® Publishing Association
Nampa, Idaho
Oshawa, Ontario, Canada
www.pacificpress.com

Design by Dennis Ferree
Cover illustration by Justinen Creative Group

Copyright 2002 by
Pacific Press® Publishing Association
All Rights Reserved.
Printed in USA.

Additional copies of this book may be purchased at
http://www.adventistbookcenter.com

ISBN: 0-8163-1918-9

02 03 04 05 06 · 5 4 3 2 1

Contents

CHAPTER 1

The Gold Mine in Kings and Chronicles

Not everyone gets excited at the opportunity to explore key themes and passages in the biblical books of Kings and Chronicles. To be honest, some people—including some Christians—think that this is about as exciting as reading through the telephone directory. They might think that reading Kings and Chronicles could be effective as a cure for insomnia, just as King Ahasuerus listened to his court records in biblical times to help him go to sleep (see Esther 6). Some consider these biblical books to be dry, boring records of the past that have little or nothing to do with the present. Too much has changed, they think, from Old Testament times to our own. We don't live under a monarchy, we live in a different part of the world, and there are other differences as well. The distance between then and now is too vast a chasm, and as a result, Kings and Chronicles have little relevance for us.

It should come as no surprise that the author of this volume does not share these sentiments. I would assume that since you are reading this book, you don't either. Far from being boring and irrelevant, Kings and Chronicles are fresh and interesting, brimming with lessons and truths applicable to God's people today. The goal of this book is to set forth some of these lessons and explore some of these truths. For those who are unconvinced of the relevance of Kings and Chronicles, let me demonstrate with the following points.

The first point is that the God of the Bible, the God of the books of Kings and Chronicles, is the same now as He was then. He declares, "For I the Lord do not change" (Malachi 3:6). He is the same "yesterday and today and forever" (Hebrews 13:8). His character is unchanged from eternity past and will remain unchanged into eternity future. As in biblical times, He is still the Lord of love, grace, and truth. He still shows mercy, showers down blessings, and metes out discipline and justice. He still yearns for His people to worship and serve Him, and when they fall short of His plan or turn away from Him altogether, as they all too often do, He still calls out for them to return to the only One who can save them.

A careful reading of Kings and Chronicles reveals that God plays a key role in the events described in these books. In other words, this history is "His story," the narrative of His dealings with humans in times past. Since He is the same today, studying these books provides insights into His ways and interactions with us.

The second point follows naturally on the heels of the unchanging nature of God. It is that human nature has not changed over the centuries either. Just as in the days of Kings and Chronicles, some people nowadays state—either by their words or their actions or both—that they believe there is no God (see Psalm 14:1). Human beings have the same inclination now as did the ancient Israelites, to disregard God's instructions, to do their own thing, and to follow their own path.

One reaction I have personally upon reading the books of Kings and Chronicles runs along these lines: Sometimes it seems that God's people today have learned very little from the past. Sometimes I feel that we have learned absolutely nothing. We make the same kinds of mistakes they did, and we make them over and over again. Now it is true that the specific way in which we turn from God might differ from the eighth century B.C. to the twenty-first century A.D. For example, by our intense preoccupation with material things, we might be worshiping the god of prosperity and wealth instead of literally bowing before a golden image as did ancient Israel. But at its core, the sin is the same. Like the people living in the days of the Israelite and Judean kings, we have forsaken "the fountain of living water, and dug out cisterns" for ourselves, "cracked cisterns that can hold no water" (Jeremiah 2:13). This being the case, we need to hear the same prophetic call to repent that was proclaimed to ancient Israel. We also need to confess our spiritual apathy and pride. We also need to seek the Lord with all our hearts (see Jeremiah 29:13).

Another point that helps demonstrate the relevance of Kings and Chronicles is the simple fact that these books are part of the record of Scripture. They comprise four of the sixty-six books of the Old and New Testaments (considering that Kings and Chronicles are each composed of two books). Since they are found within the covers of the Bible, a book inspired by God, we should assume that they are there for a purpose. Stated another way, they have a unique theological contribution to make to the message of Scripture. We ignore the teaching of these—and any other biblical books, for that matter—at our own peril. As Paul wrote, "All scripture is inspired by God and is useful for teaching, for reproof, for correction, and for training in righteousness" (2 Timothy 3:16). Kings and Chronicles are part of "all scripture," and thus they should be valued, studied, and mined for divine instruction.

Christians in general, and Adventists in particular, should be "the people of the Book." We need to study God's Word, to know what it teaches, and to apply it to our lives. The books of the Old Testament, though sometimes slighted by contemporary Christians, can speak with power and relevance to God's people today, if we will delve into them and allow the Spirit to instruct us as to their meaning. This is true of Kings and Chronicles, as well as the other thirty-five Old Testament books.

Having emphasized the relevance of Kings and Chronicles, there are several other introductory issues that deserve comment. In other words, there are some observations that should be made about these biblical books that enhance the reader's ability to understand them and their message. They also provide some insight into the perspective and approach of the present volume.

The first observation is that the books of Kings and Chronicles are among the Old Testament's historical books. This can be seen by looking at the section of the Bible in which Kings and Chronicles are found. In English translations of the Bible, Kings and Chronicles are found in the section of historical books that begins with Joshua and concludes with Esther.

It can also be seen by looking at the contents of Kings and Chronicles. These biblical books are largely taken up with recounting past events connected with the monarchies of Israel and Judah, and since history is a record of what has happened in the past, they should be considered books of history.

Some students of Scripture wonder about the accuracy of the biblical record. They ask, Did it really happen as the Bible says it did? Some also inquire whether it is really so important that the Bible be historically reliable. It is the theology of the Bible that matters, not its historical accuracy, they suggest.

Several things should be said in response. As to the historical accuracy of the Bible, time and again archaeological discoveries have corroborated the reliability of the biblical account. This is true for Kings and Chronicles, as well as for the rest of Scripture. For example, extrabiblical inscriptions have confirmed the existence of a number of Israelite and Judean kings. Both Omri and his son and successor Ahab are listed on the Moabite Stone as leaders of Israel. King Jehu of Israel is named (and probably pictured as well) on a black obelisk from Assyria. In his inscriptions, King Tiglath-pileser of Assyria refers to a number of Israelite kings bringing him tribute, including Menahem (see 2 Kings 15:19, 20), Pekah, and Hoshea. An inscription from Sennacherib parallels the biblical story (see 2 Kings 18; 19) by telling how he had Hezekiah, king of Judah, on the brink of ruin, shutting him up "like a caged bird," though as was customary for Assyrian kings, Sennacherib doesn't make any reference to the crushing defeat the Bible says eventually happened to his army (see Donald J. Wiseman, *1 and 2 Kings,* 32–35 for these and other verifications of the biblical record). All things considered, it is correct to say that Kings and Chronicles preserve an extremely reliable record of historical events.

As to whether the historical accuracy of Scripture matters or not, from a biblical perspective the answer is an unequivocal "Yes." In fact, it is not really possible to preserve the theological message of the Bible once its historicity is abandoned, because the two are closely intertwined. To diminish the Bible's history is to diminish its theology for the latter is based on the former. For instance, the theological claim that God was the Redeemer of His people Israel was based on the historical event of the redemption when He brought them out of Egyptian bondage.

A recent book expresses it this way: "The faith the Bible defines and expresses is explicitly a historical faith. It is rooted and grounded in the historicity of certain past events. Historicity is a necessary ingredient of biblical faith . . ." (Bill Arnold and Bryan Beyer, *Encountering the Old Testament,* 160, 161).

A second observation grows out of the first. While Kings and Chronicles are history, they are not merely history. They are interpreted history, or what might be better called "theological history." They do express history but with a religious viewpoint. Instead of presenting simply a sketch of events or "just the facts," as a TV detective used to ask for, these books aim to present the true meaning of these facts from a divine perspective.

This religious viewpoint is clearly visible in the theological evaluation that is given to the various kings who reigned. Some eight kings are said to have done what was right in the eyes of the Lord, though for some of them, this positive evaluation is later qualified by some mistake or an indication of a less-than-complete commitment. The other kings, including all the kings of the Northern Kingdom, are said to have done evil in the eyes of the Lord.

This religious viewpoint leads to some interesting emphases and omissions in the biblical record. Kings such as Josiah, who brought about religious revival, or Jeroboam, who was notoriously wicked, receive more attention than kings whose reigns may have been more illustrious and significant from a secular perspective. For example, the Bible takes more than six chapters to describe events that occurred during Ahab's reign (see 1 Kings 17–22), perhaps because he introduced Baal worship, which threatened to overwhelm worship of the true God during this time. By way of contrast, the Bible devotes a scant seven verses to the reign of his father Omri (see 1 Kings 16:21-28), who had some important political achievements such as the establishment of a new capital at Samaria and who was important enough that over a century later Assyrian kings were still referring to the ruling dynasty of Israel as the "house of Omri."

A third observation is related to the watershed event that happened to the nation of Israel in 930 B.C. In order to understand the narrative and structure of Kings and Chronicles, one must understand the basic fact that the ten northern tribes seceded in 930 B.C. and formed an independent kingdom, leaving the house of David ruling over only two tribes in the south. This is particularly important in understanding 1 and 2 Kings, which switches back and forth between the two kingdoms in providing its commentary and evaluation of the ruling monarchs.

A few comments distinguishing the two kingdoms are in order. The Northern Kingdom, also known as Israel, was larger in territory, having ten tribes within its boundaries. Its capital city, where the king resided, was first located at Shechem, later at Tirzah, and finally at Samaria, where it remained until Israel was destroyed as a nation.

Israel had nineteen kings (or twenty if Tibni, a rival of Omri, is counted; see 1 Kings 16:21-23) during the 208 years of its history. These kings came from nine different dynasties or ruling houses, because on a number of occasions, the ruling king was overthrown by force and killed. This feature made it impossible for the kingdom to achieve the continuity of its sister kingdom to the south. Most important from the biblical perspective, each of the kings of the Northern Kingdom did evil in the Lord's eyes, with most of them following the path of idolatry blazed by Jeroboam. In other words, there were no spiritual reformers among the kings of Israel. And finally, the Northern Kingdom met its doom in 722 B.C., when the Assyrians destroyed the capital of Samaria and carried the inhabitants away into exile (see 1 Kings 17).

The Gold Mine in Kings and Chronicles

The Southern Kingdom, also known as Judah, ruled over only the tribes of Judah and Benjamin. What it lacked in size and population, though, it more than made up for in continuity. Its capital was located at Jerusalem, which of course was the place for the divinely ordained system of worship. Each one of its nineteen kings came from the same ruling house, being descendants of David. The only exception to Davidic rule came during a six-year period during the early years of Joash, when the throne was usurped by Athaliah, the daughter of Ahab and Jezebel, who had killed her own grandchildren (see 2 Kings 11).

The Southern Kingdom outlasted the Northern Kingdom by about 136 years, finally coming to an end when Babylon destroyed Jerusalem and the temple about 586 B.C. From the biblical perspective, destruction was held at bay by the fact that the Southern Kingdom was blessed with some eight kings who are said to have done "that which was right in the eyes of the Lord," though six of them (Asa, Jehoshaphat, Joash, Amaziah, Uzziah, and Jotham) were not as complete in their commitment to purity of worship and spiritual reformation as were Hezekiah and Josiah.

Another observation concerns the pattern in which the various kings are introduced and their reigns are described in the biblical record. A literary formula is used that becomes a recurring refrain, particularly in 1 and 2 Kings. Though there is some variety, the following elements are quite common in the biblical description of the various kings.

First, there are introductory statements that appear when a king's reign is first introduced. These include a statement that synchronizes his reign with the reign of the king of the sister kingdom, be it Israel or Judah. For example, "In the twentieth year of King Jeroboam of Israel, Asa began to reign over Judah" (1 Kings 15:9). Also, the length and place of his reign (and often, for the king of Judah, his age upon coming to the throne) are given: "He [Hezekiah] was twenty-five years old when he began to reign; he reigned twenty-nine years in Jerusalem" (2 Kings 18:2). Additionally, the name of the mother is stated for most kings of Judah, as in "His [Manasseh's] mother's name was Hephzibah" (2 Kings 21:1).

After the aforementioned chronological and other information, the formula states what is perhaps the most important matter. As indicated above, the biblical author (and we don't know who wrote Kings and Chronicles, though Jeremiah is a possibility for the former and Ezra for the latter) provides a theological evaluation for each king's reign. The king is evaluated on his obedience—or disobedience—to the law of the Lord and his commitment—or lack thereof—to promoting the worship of the Lord at the temple at Jerusalem. The various kings are applauded for doing what was right or critiqued for doing what was evil in the eyes of the Lord. The following quote gives a good description of what it means to do right in God's eyes: "The judgment appears to result from an attitude of heart in full commitment, devotion, and obedience to the Lord and to His ways and word mediated through the prophets, and from a willingness to seek the Lord's will" (Wiseman, *1 and 2 Kings,* 49).

After the introductory statements, scripture moves to other achievements of the specific king under consideration and to events that transpired during his reign. Of course, there is variety here since what happened during the reigns of the various kings varied greatly. For most kings, very little is mentioned, but some like Hezekiah have several chapters devoted to their reigns.

As the Bible rounds off the discussion of a particular king, the literary formula follows more of a pattern again. There is a reference to the sources that were used in composing the written account. For example, "Now the rest of the acts of Manasseh, all that he did, and the sin that he committed, are they not written in the Book of the Annals of the Kings of Judah?" (2 Kings 21:17). Finally, there is mention of his death, burial, and successor: "Manasseh slept with his ancestors, and was buried in the garden of his house, in the garden of Uzza. His son Amon succeeded him" (2 Kings 21:18). Then, of course, the biblical author is ready to move on to the next king of the same kingdom or over to the king in the sister kingdom. Awareness of this recurring literary formula assists the reader in following and understanding the biblical presentation of the kings. (For a nice layout of this literary formula, see Beyer and Arnold, *Encountering the Old Testament,* 223.)

A final observation helpful to understanding Kings and Chronicles is to be aware of the significant role played by the prophets in these books. Though it is true that these biblical books primarily focus on the reigns of the various kings, we should notice that on some occasions the prophets are the real "movers and shakers." The prophet Elijah stands up to Ahab and 450 prophets of Baal on Mt. Carmel (see 1 Kings 18). Isaiah encourages Hezekiah with a message of victory (see 2 Kings 19). And while the significant role of these well-known prophets may not be surprising, some lesser-known prophets also played important and decisive parts in fulfilling the divine plan. Shemaiah was able to stop Rehoboam's Judah from doing battle with Jeroboam's Israel at the time of secession (see 1 Kings 12:22-24), and Huldah the prophetess declared the divine word after the finding of the book of the law in Josiah's day (see 2 Kings 22). A key element of the theological evaluation of the king revolved around his willingness or unwillingness to respond to God's messengers the prophets. This serves to call us to take God's messengers seriously today.

In conclusion, as we explore the themes and passages from Kings and Chronicles highlighted in this volume, let's remember that biblical history is not simply attempting to relate the story of people and events from the past. As indicated above, it is "His story." In other words, we should see biblical history as primarily about God, and how He worked in and through His children, and sometimes in spite of them. It is about how His people often turned away from Him to their own detriment and harm. However, He didn't abandon them forever. Though He disciplined them, His mercy endured. Through His prophets, He called repeatedly for them to return, seeking to restore them to a relationship with Himself.

And "His story" is still being written. He still calls today to each of His human children, inviting us into a relationship with Him. Though we have wandered away, we are not abandoned to our fate. The same God who declared to Israel, "I have loved you with an everlasting love" (Jeremiah 31:3), speaks the same message today.

With these thoughts in mind, we come now to some key themes and passages in the biblical books of Kings and Chronicles.

CHAPTER 2

Solomon's Finest Hour— And Yours

1 Kings 3

It was June 1940. World War II was at a critical juncture. Much was at stake. The countries of Poland, Holland, and Belgium had previously been defeated, and now France had just been devastated by the Nazi juggernaut. Britain stood alone as the major obstacle to Nazi control of Europe. In an attempt to rally the British leaders and people, Prime Minister Winston Churchill stood before Parliament and proclaimed these inspiring words:

> The Battle of France is over. I expect that the Battle of Britain is about to begin. Upon this battle depends the survival of Christian civilization. . . . Hitler knows that he will have to break us in this island or lose the war. If we can stand up to him, all Europe may be free and the life of the world may move forward into broad, sunlit uplands. But if we fail, then the whole world, including the United States, including all that we have known and cared for, will sink into the abyss of a new Dark Age, made more sinister, and perhaps more protracted, by the lights of perverted science. Let us therefore brace ourselves to our duties, and so bear ourselves that, if the British Empire and its Commonwealth last

for a thousand years, men will still say: "This was their finest hour" (Churchill, *Memoirs of the Second World War*, 326).

Churchill's stirring speech proved prophetic. Fending off the relentless German air attack, the British pilots fought skillfully and courageously and defeated an enemy that boasted superior numbers. They helped save their country. Later historians would recognize it as their finest hour.

Early in his reign, the young king Solomon had a direct encounter with God when the Lord appeared to him in a dream. His response in this divine-human encounter, together with the characteristics and attributes that he manifested, reveal Solomon at his best. Indeed, it was his finest hour. He reached his zenith right then and there. And far from being an antiquated happening in the long ago and far away, a story with no relevance for us today, this narrative challenges us to respond to God in the same way as did Solomon. It calls us to experience our finest hour.

Solomon had only been on the throne for a short time. Perhaps people were wondering about the young king. What type of leader would he turn out to be? Would he respond to the charge of his father, David, by walking in the ways of the Lord? Or would he detour from that divinely sanctioned path and turn to wicked pursuits? The jury was still out.

And perhaps Solomon wondered about himself. Maybe he had self-doubts. Was he leadership material? Did he have what it took to be king? Now that he was king and his rule had been consolidated (see 1 Kings 2), to what should he turn his attention?

At this point he made a wise decision, one that is always appropriate whenever one of God's children faces perplexing circumstances and uncertain times: He decided to engage in worship. "The king went to Gibeon to sacrifice there" (1 Kings 3:4). At that time, there was no permanent structure at which to worship for the temple had not yet been built. So Solomon journeyed to the city of Gibeon, about five miles northwest of Jerusalem, to offer sacrifices to the Lord. At Gibeon were found the bronze altar, made long ago during the days of Moses by the master artisan Bezalel, along with the wilderness tabernacle (see 2 Chronicles 1:5, 6).

While there, he had an impressive dream in which the Lord appeared to Solomon and spoke to him. This was the first of two times God appeared to him (for the other, see 1 Kings 9:1-9), and it was so profound and meaningful it should have exerted an influence on Solomon throughout his forty-year reign.

Before examining this divine manifestation and the dialogue that ensued, it is important to notice that it occurred when Solomon was engaging in acts of worship. In other words, God encountered Solomon while he was worshiping Him.

Sometimes people wonder about the presence of the Lord in their lives. "Where is God?" they inquire. "I do not sense His presence. I've never encountered Him." The example of Solomon helps underscore a significant truth: We will encounter God when we take time to worship Him. In fact, this is what worship really is all about—an encounter with the God of the universe. It involves the recognition that God really is in our midst and that we need to give all that we have and all that we are to Him. When we come to this understanding, it has the potential to transform our worship services.

Have you ever contrasted the facial expressions and demeanor of those who are at a stadium attending a sporting event with those who are attending church? The comparison is not necessarily a flattering one for church members. Whereas those at a sporting event have an attitude of vibrancy and anticipation, those at church sometimes seem unhappy and glum. (H. M. S. Richards used to remark that some churches were so cold you could ice skate down the center aisle.)

Now don't misunderstand. I'm not advocating that the same boisterousness and raucousness that characterizes the stadium should be dragged into church. However, I do believe that when God's children come to worship Him, the atmosphere should be electric with expectancy and anticipation, because we are there to encounter the Creator God of the universe who is our Lord, our Savior, and our Friend.

The invitation with which God begins the dialogue with Solomon is so vivid and memorable it bears quoting: "God said, 'Ask what I should give you'" (1 Kings 3:5). What an incredible request, coming as it did from the One who proclaims, " 'The world and all that is in it is mine' " (Psalm 50:12).

As Christmas approaches, parents sometimes say to their children, "Tell us what you really want," even though they know full well that they are unable to satisfy every desire and whim. Each year I ask the same of my two boys, now aged eleven and nine. I must be careful of what I say though, because it seems that the prices on their desires increase as my boys grow older. If the day should come when they would say, "Dad, we would like a new car for Christmas this year, one for each of us, if you don't mind," I would need to tell them they better go and find a job and start saving—unless my current salary is dramatically increased. In fairness to my boys, I should mention that they seem to recognize that Dad's resources are limited, and they don't ask for everything in the store.

But what if you should be asked what you want by Someone who possesses infinite resources? How would you respond? How did Solomon respond? Let us look carefully at Solomon's reply and break it down into its various components.

First, Solomon showed his gratitude for God's love and faithfulness that had been manifested to his father and predecessor, David. "And Solomon said, 'You have shown great and steadfast love to your servant my father David, because he walked before you in faithfulness, in righteousness, and in uprightness of heart toward you; and you have kept for him this great and steadfast love, and have given him a son to sit on his throne today'" (1 Kings 3:6). Herein we see two qualities in Solomon that are worthy of emulation: remembrance of God's past demonstrations of love and faithfulness and gratitude to God for these demonstrations.

It is worth highlighting that before Solomon filled in the blank check God had offered to him, he showed that he hadn't forgotten how God had manifested His love in the past. Unfortunately, this quality is sadly lacking among many contemporary Christians. Even though Scripture repeatedly commands us to remember God and His dealings with His people, for example, "Remember the long way that the Lord your God has led you" (Deuteronomy 8:2) and "Remember the Lord your God" (Deuteronomy 8:18)), we are all too prone to forget. We move briskly from day to day, hardly aware of how many ways in which God's kindness and grace have been manifested to us. Like Pharaoh's cupbearer who forgot about Joseph's act of kindness, we are negligent in remembering God's love to us.

It is time to change our sinful forgetfulness. It is time to, as the psalmist declares, "Remember the wonderful works he has done, his miracles, and the judgments he uttered" (Psalm 105:5). Recalling God's acts of love on our behalf provides courage to face the future. As Ellen White remarked, "As I see what the Lord has wrought, I am filled with astonishment, and with confidence in Christ as leader. We have nothing to fear for the future, except as we shall forget the way the Lord has led us, and His teaching in our past history" (*Life Sketches,* 196).

Such remembering leads to gratitude toward the Lord. Solomon was clearly grateful for God's kindness toward his family. This quality is also sadly lacking among many of us. We receive blessings from above and hasten on with hardly any acknowledgment of what God has done for us. How would we feel if our children ripped open their Christmas gifts and proceeded to play with them or wear them without any expression of thanks? How does the Lord feel when, all too often, we express no gratitude for His manifest blessings to us?

Since cleansing from sin is deliverance from a fate worse than leprosy, Jesus might well exclaim of us what He exclaimed of nine of the ten lepers whom He healed, " 'Were not all ten cleansed? Where are the other nine? Was no one found to return and give praise to God except this foreigner?' " (Luke 17:17, 18, NIV). It is worth noting that only when this one particular leper had expressed gratitude for his healing that Jesus exclaimed, " 'Your faith has made you well' " (Luke 17:19). This phrase can also be translated as, "Your faith has saved you." The same Greek word *sodzo* means "to make well" or "to save." In other words, wholeness or salvation is experienced most fully when we express our gratitude to God for His redemptive love.

The Psalms underscore the importance of expressing our gratitude to God, with entire psalms devoted to thanksgiving. For example, Psalm 136 begins and ends, using the so-called "envelope feature," with the same stirring declaration, "Give thanks to the Lord, for he is good. His love endures forever" (Psalm 136:1, 26), and in between these two bookends the psalm recounts God's great redemptive acts on behalf of Israel. The church would do well to follow this model and to come up with our own declarations of thanks, in which we state specifically and publicly how Immanuel, the God who is really with us, has worked on our behalf.

In the second part of Solomon's reply, he manifested yet another characteristic that is worthy of imitation. " 'Now, O Lord my God, you have made your servant king in place of my father David. But I am only a little child and do not know how to carry out my duties' "(1 Kings 3:7, NIV). By making reference to his own youth, inexperience, and his lack of ability, Solomon was modeling a humility that is needed—and sometimes lacking—among Christians today.

"I'm so young," he declared. "I know so little. Why, I don't even know how to go out or come in" (which is a literal translation of the Hebrew). In saying this, Solomon is emphasizing his lack of dependence on self and his complete dependence on God.

Often when Christians feel called to do a work for God, they rush ahead in their own strength, and this is their downfall. The example of Moses is instructive here. When he was forty years old, he thought the time for Israel's freedom had come (see Acts 7:23-28). He thought it was time to strike a blow for God. And he thought he was just the man to do it! After all, he was an Egyptian prince. He had been trained in leadership techniques. He had learned military skills. Who better than him to lead God's people? But when he tried to step forward in his own strength and wisdom, his efforts collapsed and he had to flee from Egypt (see Exodus 2:11-15). Ironically, he is an agent of deliverance, but instead of delivering an entire nation, he saves a group of ladies from some bullying shepherds (see Exodus 2:16, 17).

The truth is, Moses had some things to learn—or perhaps we should say unlearn—before he was ready to be the type of leader God wanted him to be. Once he had spent forty years in the wilderness, learning dependence on God and unlearning reliance on self, then and only then was he ready for the divine commission to deliver the Lord's people.

Sometimes as Christians we are like Elijah following his triumph on Mt. Carmel. We think of ourselves as the ones standing in the breach, providing the spiritual leadership that is sorely needed. We consider ourselves as spiritually strong and as the only ones who are truly committed. We might even wonder inwardly—though of course we would be careful not to phrase it this way—what God and His cause would do without our talents. At these times, we need to have our self broken, just as Elijah did (see 1 Kings 19). We need to be reminded that God doesn't need us nearly as much as we need Him. We need to remember what Paul affirmed so eloquently, "When I am weak, then I am strong" (2 Corinthians 12:10, NIV). We need to join Solomon is declaring, " 'I am only a little child and do not know how to carry out my duties' " (1 Kings 3:7, NIV). We need to drop to our knees, be purged of self, and be filled with Christ.

There is yet a third part of Solomon's reply that is worth our attention. After mentioning God's acts of kindness and his own insufficiency, Solomon finally responded to God's invitation, " 'Ask for whatever you want me to give you' " (1 Kings 3:5, NIV). What did he request? Many offspring? Wealth? Worldwide fame? A lengthy reign? No, none of the above. In what I imagine to be an expression-filled voice, Solomon pleaded, " 'Give your servant a discerning heart to govern your people and to distinguish between right and wrong' " (1 Kings 3:9, NIV).

In the original Hebrew, a "discerning heart" is literally a "listening heart," or it can also be translated "an obedient heart." It is theologically significant that in the Old Testament the same word (*shama*) is used for "listening" and "obeying" (see Paul House, *1, 2 Kings,* 110). In biblical thought, to listen to God is to obey, and the one who doesn't obey hasn't truly listened.

Solomon recognized his need to listen to the voice of God. Only then would he have the wisdom and discernment that he needed for governing. Only then would he be able to, as the text says, " 'distinguish between right and wrong' " (1 Kings 3:9, NIV).

Of all the things needed by God's people today, next to an experience of God's forgiving and transforming grace and a manifestation of His love in our midst, our greatest need is of spiritual discernment. We often make shortsighted and misguided choices. We neglect to make spiritual matters a priority. We indulge in entertainment practices that draw us away from Christ instead of toward Him. Our eyes have adjusted to the moral darkness around us, and we cannot distinguish right from wrong.

The remedy for this plight is God's gift of discernment, the spiritual wisdom that comes from having a listening heart. At this juncture in earth's history, we must recognize this great need. We must echo the plea of Solomon, "Please, Lord, give me discernment. Give me a listening heart."

Of course, it takes time for the heart to listen to God, just as it takes time for us to listen to a friend. It may mean rearranging our schedules, readjusting our priorities. But the gain is more than worth the effort. It is nothing other than the fellowship with God that is a foretaste of the eternal future that He wants to share with us.

The remainder of 1 Kings 3 describes how Solomon manifested this discernment in a remarkable way, solving the thorny dilemma of the baby claimed by two different women (see 1 Kings 3:16-28). His wisdom caused everyone to marvel. But in a way, what proceeded to happen was simply what was to be expected once God's wisdom was granted. It was simply the natural outflow of events. The climax of the chapter, Solomon's finest hour, was the moment he remembered with gratitude God's kindness and love, manifested humility, and expressed an earnest plea to be granted a heart that listened to the voice of God.

Gratitude, humility, a prayer for a listening heart—all are called for today. In fact, Christians can experience their finest hour through these characteristics, just as did Solomon. The reason this is true is that whatever happens later in one's life, there can be no finer moment than one in which we are grateful to God, when we humble ourselves before Him, and beseech Him to grant that we might continue to listen to His voice and so gain spiritual discernment.

As we continue to manifest these characteristics, our finest hour will be an ongoing experience instead of a one-time event. We will move from victory to victory. Sad to say, this didn't occur with Solomon. The tragedy of 1 Kings is that the event occurred early in his reign and was not a lifelong experience. As the next chapter will show, the humility was forgotten and the listening heart stopped listening. His finest hour was merely an hour. What a tragedy! But it doesn't have to be that way with us, as long as we maintain a listening heart.

CHAPTER 3

It Might Have Been

1 Kings 4-11

Both his pedigree and his résumé are extremely impressive. At first glance, one would expect him to be among the foremost of America's founding fathers. He was the grandson of the famous theologian Jonathan Edwards and the son of the president of Princeton College (later Princeton University). He served as a soldier in the Revolutionary War and spent some time as an officer on the staff of George Washington. Later he was chosen as a United States senator from the state of New York, and his political star was on the rise. He did well as a national candidate in the election of 1800, coming within one electoral vote of being elected President in this hotly disputed contest, before finally settling for the vice-presidency under Thomas Jefferson.

Had his public life ended before 1804, the name of Aaron Burr would have been spoken with respect and honor instead of disdain and contempt. But after mortally wounding Alexander Hamilton in their celebrated pistol duel and then conspiring with the British to set up an independent government west of the Mississippi River, he came to be considered in the same vein as the likes of Benedict Arnold. Names like scoundrel, traitor, and worse were applied to him. Not even a verdict of not guilty at his trial for treason could clear his tarnished reputation.

23

Instead of being remembered fondly as an honored leader of our infant country, he was remembered for his acts of villainy.

The mournful words of John Greenleaf Whittier seem applicable to the despised Burr:

"Of all sad words of tongue or pen,

The saddest are these:

'It might have been.' "

(*Maude Miller.* Stanza 53)

This poignant saying is also relevant to the life of King Solomon. He could have been remembered for his leadership in building the temple of the Lord and for his marvelous prayer during the dedication ceremonies. He could have been remembered for highlighting the truth that temporal blessings are not an end in themselves but a means by which to draw others to worship the Giver of every good and perfect gift. The lasting memory of Solomon could have been that of one whose divinely bestowed wisdom enabled him to bring glory to the true God, the Lord of Israel.

And while he was known for all these and more, the last chapter dealing with his life in 1 Kings sounds a tragic note that casts a shadow over all of these other memories: "King Solomon loved many foreign women. . . . For when Solomon was old, his wives turned away his heart after other gods" (1 Kings 11:1, 4). Yes, the lingering image of Solomon in 1 Kings is of a feeble, compromising monarch who, though he ruled a vast swath of territory from the Euphrates to the border of Egypt (see 1 Kings 4:21), was unable to rule the passions that surged in his own heart. And though as the book of Ecclesiastes suggests, he did repent before his life came to an end (see also *Prophets and Kings,* pp. 77–80), he was not able to repair the damage that had been done to the spiritual and moral fabric of the nation. The epitaph on Solomon's tombstone could well be Whittier's words, "It might have been."

Before exploring Solomon's straying from God, though, it is appropriate (and only fair to Solomon!) to consider some of his earlier and more noble feats. In the fourth year of his reign (see 1 Kings 6:1) around

966 B.C., he began the construction of a temple for the Lord. Though not a large building (the main shrine was only about 90 feet long, 30 feet wide, and 45 feet high; see 1 Kings 6:2), it was exquisitely decorated and furnished, truly a palace befitting the Creator God of the universe. It took seven years and a huge workforce to complete this project (see 1 Kings 5:13-16; 6:38).

Upon completion, Solomon presided at the dedication of this edifice. A beautiful and thrilling scene is described. After the ark of the covenant containing the Ten Commandments had been placed in the Most Holy Place of the new temple, God favored the occasion with His presence. "And when the priests came out of the holy place, a cloud filled the house of the Lord, so that the priests could not stand to minister because of the cloud; for the glory of the Lord filled the house of the Lord" (1 Kings 8:10, 11). The same glorious cloud that filled the wilderness tabernacle in Moses' time (see Exodus 40:34) now dwelt in the Jerusalem temple. God was present at His house.

Do God's modern-day children recognize that the same reality is still true today? Though we may not see a glorious cloud or hear a sound like a rushing, mighty wind as on Pentecost (see Acts 2:2), the Lord is just as present among His people when they meet to worship His name as He was in ancient times (see Matthew 18:20). God is truly there. He is still Immanuel, "God with us." If we know and cherish this truth, it whets our appetite to be at the place of worship.

As part of the dedication ceremony, Solomon stood in front of the entire congregation, spread out his hands toward heaven, and prayed a magnificent dedicatory prayer, which is recorded in 1 Kings 8:23-61. (To receive inspiration from four of the greatest prayers of the Old Testament, read Ezra 9, Nehemiah 9, and Daniel 9 in addition to Solomon's prayer in 1 Kings 8.) This prayer is an exemplary prayer in many respects and includes several elements that are worth highlighting.

First, Solomon engaged in praise and adoration of God, declaring, " 'O Lord, God of Israel, there is no God like you in heaven above or on earth beneath' " (1 Kings 8:23). Some may wonder, Why do human beings need to praise God? Is it just a way to feed the divine ego? Does God's self-esteem need building up? No, that isn't the issue. While God does love to hear expressions of appreciation from His children, just as human parents do, the praise and adoration are more for our benefit than His. In fact, we are lifted up spiritually when we become channels of praise and adoration to God. There is something inherently ennobling in the experience. An attitude of praise toward God brings us into harmony with the reality of the universe.

Second, Solomon thanked God for fulfilling His promises in the past (see 1 Kings 8:24) and called on Him to be faithful to His promises in the future (see 1 Kings 8:25, 26). Recognition of God's faithfulness to His promises and claiming these promises for the future are still important elements of prayer, elements, unfortunately, that are sometimes overlooked. God is still faithful to His word. He still keeps His promises. What Joshua said many centuries ago is just as true today: " 'Not one thing has failed of all the good things that the Lord your God promised concerning you; all have come to pass for you, not one of them has failed' " (Joshua 23:14). But we sometimes get so involved in the hustle and bustle of our daily activities that we neglect to notice the various and sundry ways in which God has been faithful to keep His word.

As for the future, the Lord never tires of being reminded of His promises. Though sometimes earthly parents may become annoyed when their children remind them of something they have said, it is not so with God. There are occasions when my own sons frustrate me by quoting my own lips. "But, Dad, you said we could go to the park today," they might say. And I might reply, somewhat annoyed, "But I didn't know it was going to be raining," or "I didn't know that we were going to have company." No, I don't always like to be reminded of my own words.

But it isn't that way with God. Since His word endures forever (see Isaiah 40:8), He is always willing for us to claim it in prayer and to cling to it in our lives.

A third element worth noting in Solomon's magnificent prayer is its emphasis on sin, repentance, and forgiveness. Solomon had remarkably clear insight into the reality of the human condition. Speaking to God about the people of Israel, he said, " 'If they sin against you—for there is no one who does not sin' " (1 Kings 8:46). He knew the shortcomings of his people, and he knew his own flaws. Long before the New Testament recognition of universal human sinfulness (see Romans 3:23), Solomon declared the same truth.

But the story doesn't end with human sinfulness. Solomon moved on to the next stage. " 'If they repent with all their heart and soul' " (1 Kings 8:48). Yes, Israel would sin. Solomon anticipated it. The seeds of rebellion were there, even on that high day of celebration when the temple was dedicated. But Solomon also anticipated that Israel would "return" or "turn back" to God, which is the literal meaning of the Hebrew word for repentance. Their sin would lead them away, but they would return.

There is yet one more stage to mention, for according to Solomon's prayer, the matter doesn't end with human repentance either. In fact, it doesn't end with human action at all. In the context of praying about Israel's future sin and repentance, Solomon pleaded with God, "Forgive Your people who have sinned against You, and all their transgressions that they have committed against You." The focus on forgiveness in Solomon's prayer is intense. Five times in his moving prayer he called on God to forgive His people when they turned to Him in repentance (see 1 Kings 8:30, 34, 36, 39, 50).

Recognition of our status as sinners, understanding our need for repentance, embracing the wonderful gift of God's forgiveness—all were key elements in Solomon's prayer, and they are vital in our prayer lives and in our reception of the gift of salvation today. In a sense, his prayer is a proclamation of the gospel right there in Old Testament times.

However, notwithstanding Solomon's great achievements and his profound prayer, the truth of the matter is that his reign never accomplished all it could have from a divine perspective. The Bible's assessment of Solomon during the closing years of his reign is not a positive one: "Then the Lord was angry with Solomon, because his heart had turned away from the Lord, the God of Israel, who had appeared to him twice, and had commanded him concerning this matter, that he should not follow other gods; but he did not observe what the Lord commanded" (1 Kings 11:9, 10). It is true that Solomon amassed tremendous wealth and achieved widespread fame (see 1 Kings 10:21-27), but in the balances of heaven he was weighed and found wanting, for "his heart was not true to the Lord his God" (1 Kings 11:4).

I would like to offer some observations on Solomon's turning away from God in the hope that in understanding his mistake we may be able to avoid repeating it. As one philosopher said, "Those who do not remember the past are condemned to repeat it."

The first observation is that Solomon's movement away from God began when he violated the express command of God. Through his servant Moses, the Lord had warned that the king who would reign over Israel "must not acquire many wives for himself, or else his heart will turn away; also silver and gold he must not acquire in great quantity for himself" (Deuteronomy 17:17). Solomon was well acquainted with Deuteronomy. Evidence for this is found in the fact that his words and prayer in 1 Kings 8 "contain fifty-nine instances of phrases and language parallel to Deuteronomy phraseology" (Hamilton, *Handbook on the Historical Books,* 380). But though he liked to quote Deuteronomy, he was unwilling to do what really mattered: follow its counsels in his own life. Notwithstanding the divine prohibition on marrying many wives, Solomon's harem was bulging with 1,000 wives and concubines (see 1 Kings 11:3). Despite the prescription against amassing great quantities of silver and gold, Solomon accumulated as much of these precious metals as he possibly could (see 1 Kings 10:23-25).

Perhaps he thought he was strong enough spiritually to withstand the temptations that would come with excessive riches and multiple wives. Maybe he thought the commands of Deuteronomy applied to lesser kings than himself, or perhaps he just paid little attention to them. But for whatever reason, he clearly disobeyed God's word and his disobedience came at a steep price.

But to be faithful to Scripture we must recognize that Solomon's express violation of God's command is not as important now as our own disobedience. Each of us must ask the question, In what ways am I disregarding God's Word and violating His commands? What am I doing that I know to be in conflict with the Word of God? Whatever area of my life it may involve, whether entertainment practices, use of my time or resources, or anything else, it will diminish my connection with God.

Now it may take a while for the tragic results of my disobedience to be obvious and apparent in my life. Interestingly enough, early in his reign Solomon made an alliance with Pharaoh by marrying his daughter (1 Kings 3:1). Though this was an acceptable practice in its day and must have seemed like a shrewd geo-political maneuver, it was a violation of God's intention regarding the marriage choices of His people (see Deuteronomy 7:3). It is a bad omen for what will occur later during the reign of Solomon. Though unseen to the casual observer, termites of disobedience are eroding his spiritual foundation. Such is always the case when we violate the express will of God.

A second observation concerns the danger of material possessions. As his reign progressed, material possessions played an increasingly prominent role in Solomon's life. In fact, a careful reading of 1 Kings 10:14-29 suggests that material possessions were a preoccupation with him. They came to dominate his existence and to play a role in turning him away from God.

Perhaps his priorities had been out of kilter earlier in his reign on this issue as well. Bible students often note and applaud the elaborate preparations and immense labor that went into building the Lord's temple. They sometimes commend Solomon for his Herculean efforts. But a careful comparison of 1 Kings 6:38 and 1 Kings 7:1 (note that the verses were juxtaposed in the original Hebrew because it had no chapter and verse divisions) highlights the fact that Solomon spent nearly twice as much time on his own palace as on the temple!

Perhaps Solomon had not yet learned the truth Jesus would later articulate: "Seek ye first the kingdom of God and his righteousness"

(Matthew 6:33, KJV). And perhaps we haven't either. Despite the biblical warnings against materialism, despite the examples of biblical individuals such as Balaam and Achan whose greed and covetousness cost them everything, God's children today still pine for more in the way of material possessions. We are correct when we say that money is not the root of all evil, it's the love of money (see 1 Tim. 6:10). However, we fail to mention that it is all too often the case that when we have an abundance of money we tend to love it as well.

Material possessions can even be a distraction to the corporate Church if viewed as an end in themselves. Sometimes Church members, when asked to describe the ways in which God has blessed His people, start listing the Church's possessions. They mention educational institutions, hospitals, publishing houses, and the like. As helpful as these can be in fulfilling the Church's mission, they are not the greatest asset of the Church. Not even close to it! The greatest asset of the Church is the single individual who will yield himself or herself entirely to the Lord to accomplish His work on the earth. It is the single person who will turn his or her talents over completely to God in order to lift up Jesus and bring glory to His name. We must never forget this.

One day Solomon would learn that material possessions cannot provide happiness. They are not an end in themselves. In fact, he realized that to try to use them to provide satisfaction and fulfillment in life leaves one empty and hollow (see Ecclesiastes 2:1-11). Our lives will be far better if we learn that sooner rather than later.

A final observation worth making on Solomon's apostasy is that most of all it was a matter of the heart. His heart was not where it should have been. Notice the emphasis on this in Scripture. In 1 Kings 11:4, we read, "His wives turned away his heart after other gods; and his heart was not true to the Lord his God." A few verses later the Bible declares of Solomon, "His heart had turned away from the Lord" (1 Kings 11:9).

It would not be incorrect to say that Solomon's worst problem of all was a heart problem. While he had problems in his married life, polygamist that he was, and while he had problems with materialism, these weren't his worst problem. No, the worst problem was the one with his heart. Not a leaky heart valve, not an irregular heartbeat, but heart problems nonetheless. His heart, a term that connoted his level of spiritual commitment, his focus in life, his time, talents, and energies, was not where it should have been. Like the church of Ephesus centuries later (see Revelation 2:4), Solomon had lost his first love because his heart was turned away from God.

And what might be said of us on this matter? It doesn't matter whether we were baptized five months ago, five years ago, or fifty years ago. The relevant question is, Where is our heart today? Where is our focus in life? Who or what has pride of place on our pyramid of commitments?

Someone might ask, How can I tell? The following quote from *Steps to Christ* provides one of the clearest answers I have found to this question. Notice the criteria laid down for determining where our hearts are: "Who has the heart? With whom are our thoughts? Of whom do we love to converse? Who has our warmest affections and our best energies? If we are Christ's, our thoughts are with Him, and our sweetest thoughts are of Him. All we have and are is consecrated to Him. We long to bear His image, breathe His spirit, do His will, and please Him in all things" (Ellen G. White, *Steps to Christ*, 58).

"It might have been." Tragically, these words are all too relevant in describing Solomon—a man with a special endowment of wisdom, a king whose reign held such bright promise. He was one who could have been known as a beacon of light and truth throughout the world, one who could have had the leaders of the world saying with awe, as did the Queen of Sheba, " 'Blessed be the Lord your God' " (1 Kings 10:9). All this might have been, but for the problem of Solomon's straying heart.

"It might have been." Words applicable to Aaron Burr. Words applicable to Solomon. Will they be applicable to you?

CHAPTER

Heading the Wrong Way

1 Kings 12

My wife, Mary, still identifies it as her moment of supreme glory on the athletic field. But when you read about it, you might be surprised that she doesn't choose to omit it when she recites her achievements in life.

It happened on a sunny afternoon during her academy days in southern California. Her class was playing football during physical education that day. It would probably be correct to say that this sport was not one at which my wife really excelled. My wife's team was on defense when suddenly, something happened that would long be remembered by the other players and that my wife still remembers today.

The quarterback of the other team had called a passing play. But what he didn't reckon with was my wife's defensive skills. He flung his pass into the air toward his intended receiver, but she stepped into the path of the ball and intercepted it. Holding the ball tightly, she took off running for the end zone. It was an exciting moment for her since it was rather rare for her to make an interception.

Her exploit was also causing a stir among the other players. As she raced across the goal line, she could hear her teammates shouting excitedly at her, "Go, Mary, go!" Or at least that's what she thought they were saying, for in actuality they were yelling, "No, Mary, no!" Unfortunately for Mary and her teammates, she had run the wrong direction and her wrong-way run for a safety earned two points for the other team.

I have pointed out to my wife that she is not the only one to be known for such a dubious feat. In 1964 Jim Marshall of the Minnesota Vikings scooped up a fumble and rumbled sixty-six yards into the end zone before being tackled. The only problem was, it was the wrong end zone, and he also netted two points for the other team. Even though Marshall would go on to be a superb defenseman for the Vikings and would even set the record for consecutive games played, he would never live down his *faux pas*. Forever, he would be known as the man who ran the wrong way on a recovered fumble.

While the above two incidents demonstrate how it can be humorous to go the wrong way in an athletic contest, heading the wrong way can be dangerous in other areas of life. One of my teaching colleagues almost had a head-on collision with an inebriated driver on a nearby highway. She was driving in the wrong direction for the lane she was in. When I served as a guest lecturer in England several years ago, it was a challenge to get accustomed to driving on the left side of the road. I don't think I can really say that I ever got used to it. It was as though a magnet naturally pulled me over to the right side. I can remember my wife saying to me, "Greg, you're on the wrong side. You're going the wrong way for this lane."

If it is dangerous to have a driver heading the wrong way, for someone to be driving on the wrong side of the road, it is even more perilous for an entire nation to proceed in the wrong direction. Yet this is just what happened in the Northern Kingdom of Israel. Through some profound spiritual blunders he made, Jeroboam, the very first king, got the nation heading the wrong way. His example is one of the worst examples of leading people spiritually astray found in the entire Bible. Additionally, it would be a mistake from which the Northern Kingdom of Israel would never recover.

It is nearly impossible to overstate the importance of Jeroboam's sin from a biblical perspective. To demonstrate the significance of his sin and its baleful influence on the people, it is only necessary to read the two books of Kings and take note of how the name Jeroboam is used. The name Jeroboam appears seventy times in the books of 1 and 2 Kings. While sometimes the Bible describes something Jeroboam did during his reign, many of these references use Jeroboam as a negative standard of comparison for his successors on the throne. In fact, of the eighteen kings who followed Jeroboam on the throne of the Northern Kingdom, all but three are said to either walk in Jeroboam's sin or to not turn away from Jeroboam's sin (Hamilton, *Handbook on the Historical Books*, 420).

For example, speaking of Ahaziah, the Bible proclaims, "He did what was evil in the sight of the Lord, and walked in the way of his father and mother, and in the way of Jeroboam son of Nebat, who caused Israel to sin" (1 Kings 22:52). And later, when referring to Jehoram, the Bible declares, "Nevertheless he clung to the sin of Jeroboam son of Nebat, which he caused Israel to commit; he did not depart from it" (2 Kings 3:3). In other words, because he was the first king of Israel whose evil acts got the nation heading the wrong way, Jeroboam is a fitting paradigm of evil from the biblical perspective.

But what spiritual blunders did he commit? What did he really do to lead the people of Israel astray, to get them heading the wrong way? This matter needs to be addressed, for understanding the mistakes through which Jeroboam led the people astray back then will enable us to avoid the same blunders now. It will enable us to avoid going astray from God in our own lives as well as to keep from leading others away. To these mistakes we now turn.

The first blunder made by Jeroboam upon becoming king was that he didn't trust God to be faithful to what He had promised. To understand this blunder, let's review the record of events. The year was about 930 B.C. Upon the death of Solomon, some of the leaders of Israel came to his son Rehoboam and asked for some relief from the hard service

Solomon had demanded (see 1 Kings 12:3-4). Evidently, many people had felt oppressed because of heavy taxation and required labor.

Rehoboam sought advice from two groups. The older and more mature advisors who had attended his father counseled him to reply gently to the request of the people and to try and accommodate them (see 1 Kings 12:5-7). But his other counselors advised differently. The kids with whom he had grown up (though most versions give a translation like "young men," the Hebrew word used here [*yeladim*] literally means "children," perhaps indicating their immaturity and the foolishness of their advice; see 1 Kings 12:9,10) told him, in essence, to show the petitioners who was boss (see 1 Kings 12:10, 11). According to them, this was no time to show weakness.

Unwisely, Rehoboam followed the advice of the "kids"—and he paid a heavy price. The ten northern tribes revolted, leaving Rehoboam to rule over only the tribes of Judah and Benjamin (see 1 Kings 12:23). The other tribes chose Jeroboam and crowned him as a rival king (see 1 Kings 12:20).

Now from a biblical perspective, this "surprising" turn of events was not so surprising after all. In fact, it was only to be expected. While Solomon was still alive, the prophet Ahijah had encountered Jeroboam one day and startled him by announcing that because of Solomon's idolatry, God was going to sunder his kingdom and place ten of the tribes under Jeroboam's rule (see 1 Kings 11:29-33). To symbolize what would take place, Ahijah had even ripped up the new garment he was wearing into twelve pieces and had handed ten of them to Jeroboam. Furthermore, another prophet, Shemaiah by name, reinforced Ahijah's prophetic message once the revolt had taken place. In warning Rehoboam not to use armed force in an attempt to bring the northern tribes back under his rule, he declared that the turn of events was from the Lord (see 1 Kings 12:24).

The main point in what I have been saying is that God had promised Jeroboam he would rule over ten tribes of Israel. He had pledged in advance of the fact that Jeroboam would become king. Yet hardly had

Jeroboam become king than he said to himself, " 'Now the kingdom may well revert to the house of David' " (1 Kings 12:26).

In this brief statement we see Jeroboam's first major mistake. He didn't trust in God's word. He didn't have confidence that God would be faithful to His promise. Notwithstanding the fact that God had promised him that he would rule over ten tribes, notwithstanding the fact that God had fulfilled His word thus far and Jeroboam was reigning as king, he was troubled by the thought that these same tribes would get rid of him and return to Rehoboam as their king. He didn't trust God's promise, and his lack of trust would be forever reflected in his people.

In fairness to Jeroboam, we must say that he is not alone in the biblical record. A number of other people made the same mistake and thus headed in the wrong direction. The disciple Judas doubted that Jesus would fulfill His promise to usher in God's kingdom, so he decided on a strategy to force Jesus' hand and leave Him with no choice but to set Himself up as king. During their journey through the wilderness, the Israelites repeatedly doubted whether God would be faithful to His promise to take care of their needs and bring them to the land of Canaan. And going back to the very beginning of human history, it was this same seed of doubt that sprouted in the hearts of Adam and Eve and led them to give in to the serpent's temptation.

What about God's people today? What about you and me? The Lord has given us some "precious and very great promises" (2 Peter 1:4). Some of the most valuable of these promises are that He will never leave us nor forsake us (see Hebrews 13:5), that He has a wonderful plan for our lives (see Jeremiah 29:11), and that He will come again and take us to the place He has prepared for us (see John 14:1-3).

How do we respond when challenges and difficulties come in life? Do we, like Jeroboam, doubt God's promises? Or do we have confidence and peace because we know that the Lord has promised to be faithful to His word (see Matt. 24:35). Whenever we doubt God's promises, we are heading the wrong way.

A second blunder made by Jeroboam in the infancy of his reign and his nation is related to and grows out of the first. He was overly concerned about the future. He was worried about what tomorrow held. Since he didn't trust God's promise, he became anxious about what was going to happen and said to himself, " 'If this people continues to go up to offer sacrifices in the house of the Lord at Jerusalem, the heart of this people will turn again to their master, King Rehoboam of Judah; they will kill me and return to King Rehoboam of Judah' " (1 Kings 12:27).

As we will see below, when he became overly anxious about the future, he began making bad decisions in the present. Because of his excessive worry and anxiety, he led his entire nation in the wrong direction.

The mistake of being overly worried about the future is not limited to the ancient world. Despite the clear admonition of Jesus in the Sermon on the Mount, " 'Do not worry about tomorrow' " (Matthew 6:34), often God's children are concerned and anxious about what is going to happen. We worry about questions like the following: Will we get the job that we want so badly? Will our children experience a happy life and marriage? Will they stay in the church? Will our health remain good? Will we return safely from our business trip? And the questions and concerns go on *ad infinitum.*

Now the Bible does not teach us that we should never give time and thought to engaging in appropriate planning for the future. If I need to fly somewhere for a speaking appointment, it would be ill-advised—not to mention exorbitantly expensive—to just wander down to the airport with no ticket on the day I need to depart and find out if there are any seats available. What the Bible does teach us is that we should not worry about the future. The reason why worry is unnecessary is that we are called to place the things about the future that would otherwise cause us anxiety into the hands of a Sovereign God who loves us with an infinite love and has an intense interest in us.

But how should we handle it when worries crop up, as they will in all of our lives? What should we do when excessive anxiety sends us careening the wrong way? I can remember a time some months ago when I was extremely concerned about something. I was worried about it to the point that it dominated my thinking, interfering with my ability to concentrate on other activities such as reading the Word of God. And to make matters worse, the day that this anxiety was overwhelming me was the Sabbath. Though it was the seventh day of the week and I wasn't working per se, due to my worries I wasn't really keeping Sabbath in my heart.

I dropped to my knees and asked God to give a sense of calm and to bless me with His gentle peace. I confessed my anxiety, and asked Him to grant me a Sabbath rest within. And He answered. No, I didn't hear an audible voice, there was no light in the sky, but it was as though He said, "Peace, peace, I give you peace in your life." So what is the antidote to worry? It is found on our knees, in relationship with God. As Paul exclaimed, "The peace of God, which surpasses all understanding, will guard your hearts and minds in Christ Jesus" (Philippians 4:7).

A third blunder made by Jeroboam was that he repeated past mistakes. He neglected to learn the lessons from Israel's past. The Bible states, "So the king took counsel, and made two calves of gold. He said to the people, 'You have gone up to Jerusalem long enough. Here are your gods, O Israel, who brought you up out of the land of Egypt.' He set one in Bethel, and the other he put in Dan. And this thing became a sin, for the people went to worship before the one at Bethel and before the other as far as Dan" (1 Kings 12:28-30).

The careful student of Scripture is aware that this same idea has been tried before, with nearly identical words being used by the one promoting worship of the golden calf, and with equally tragic results. "He [Aaron] took the gold from them, formed it in a mold, and cast an image of a calf; and they said, 'These are your gods, O Israel, who brought you up out of the land of Egypt' " (Exodus 32:4).

In light of the sad outcome of Israel's worship of the golden calf at Sinai, with the Ten Commandments lying in pieces on the ground and the desert sand soaking up Israelite blood (see Exodus 32:19, 25-28), it is astonishing to think that Jeroboam would encourage the same kind of worship and even use Aaron's words to introduce his innovation. But he did nonetheless, and it caused his nation to head the wrong way. As a nation, Israel never got back on the right path. It never recovered. As pointed out above, this sin in which Jeroboam led the people is stated in Scripture to be the cause of their ongoing estrangement from God and eventual national ruin.

While we may be astonished at Jeroboam's course of action, if truth were told, we are sometimes his spiritual descendants. We are amazingly slow at learning from the past, both from the biblical stories and the lessons available in our own lives. We neglect to remember that "these things happened to them [Israelites] to serve as an example, and they were written down to instruct us, on whom the ends of the ages have come" (1 Corinthians 10:11). We repeat the same mistakes that Israel did, or the same ones that our parents or grandparents did. As one wit said, "The only thing that we learn from history is that we learn nothing from history."

The only way to break this pattern of repeated past mistakes, the only way to break free from the mold, as did kings like Hezekiah and Josiah who came after wicked fathers but who chose a righteous path, is by responding to the grace of God. It is by living out in one's life the declaration of Paul, "I can do all things through Him who strengthens me" (Philippians 4:13).

The fourth blunder made by Jeroboam that turned his people the wrong way occurred when he called the Israelites away from a complete and wholehearted commitment to God. In an attempt to dissuade them from going to the temple and to entice them to worship the golden calves at Dan and Bethel, he told them, " 'It is too much for you to go up to Jerusalem' " (1 Kings 12:28, NIV).

This is an interesting attempt at persuasion. Exactly what "too much" meant to Jeroboam we do not know. It could have been speaking of the distance, implying that it was too far. He might have been referring to the effort required to travel so far or the costliness of the trip. But whatever he meant by this term, its persuasive effects were successful, for "this thing became a sin, for the people went to worship before the one at Bethel and before the other as far as Dan" (1 Kings 12:30).

The people of Israel should have known better. They were aware that the true God asked for a complete commitment, He required them to love Him with all their heart and soul and might (see Deuteronomy 6:5). Thus, they should have known that any one suggesting that whatever amount of time, money, or effort spent in worshiping God was "too much" was leading them the wrong way.

Unfortunately, though God's people should know better today, our actions don't always indicate it. We sometimes listen to voices that call us to something less than a complete commitment. Voices that tell us that it is "too much" to be faithful in our tithes and offerings. Voices that say that the sacrifice is "too much" if one turns down a lucrative job that would require Sabbath work. Voices that tell us God expects "too much" when He asks us to be sexually pure.

As Paul warned it would, the time has arrived when "people will not put up with sound doctrine, but having itching ears, they will accumulate for themselves teachers to suit their own desires" (2 Timothy 4:3). In other words, we sometimes gravitate toward spiritual leaders who tell us what we want to hear, what makes us feel good, instead of what we need to hear. The story of Jeroboam shouts out this warning: Beware of anyone who would turn you away from a complete commitment to God, for that person is pointing you in the wrong way.

As mentioned above, there is a sad outcome to the story of Jeroboam. His spiritual blunders got his nation and its kings heading in the wrong direction, and they never did an about-face. They never got back on track. You can read 1 and 2 Kings in their entirety. Of the nineteen kings of the Northern Kingdom (twenty if Tibni is included; see 1 Kings 16:21-22), every last one of them did evil in the Lord's sight. Not one reforming king was among them.

In the final analysis, though, what is important now is not which way ancient Israel, misled by the faithless and sinful Jeroboam, was heading. The vital question for us is, Which way are we headed?

40

CHAPTER 5

Get Off the Fence

1 Kings 18

Gary had a problem. He had a big problem. He had a huge, gigantic problem. He was sitting on the fence, trying to maintain a special friendship with two different young ladies. In other words, he had two girlfriends. Now before continuing his story, let's make sure it is clear what the phrase "sitting on the fence" means. A fence sitter is someone who can't quite decide which side to be on, someone who vacillates, someone who goes back and forth between one position and another. In other words, it is someone who wants to have it both ways. A fence sitter is someone who can't make up his or her mind. And Gary was a fence sitter *par excellence!*

First, there had been Janet. Gary had begun dating Janet during his first year at college. The relationship had prospered throughout that year and even continued—mainly because of Janet's faithfulness in writing letters and sending care packages from home—during the next year when Gary was serving in the Pacific Islands as a student missionary.

When Gary returned from the islands to continue his education, he was disappointed that Janet would be continuing her studies at another campus. However, they pledged to keep the relationship going and to keep in touch through letters and phone calls.

But no sooner was Gary back at college than he began to notice some of the beautiful "scenery" around campus. It seemed as though all the flowers had blossomed during his time away. Perhaps a year on an isolated island had heightened his awareness, but for whatever reason, he began forming a special relationship with Becky, one of the prettiest of those blooming flowers. Nothing was inherently wrong with the relationship, except for the fact that Gary did not tell Becky that he was supposed to be dating Janet, nor did he tell Janet about his new girlfriend Becky. He thought about it, but when he considered ending things with Janet, he felt like a heel. He squirmed inwardly. Janet had written him faithfully during his year in the Pacific, and after all, she was a very lovely girl. What if things didn't work out with Becky? What's wrong with a little "relationship insurance" anyway?

So what did he do? He sat on the fence. He vacillated. He tried to have it both ways. And it worked too, at least for a little while. He was able to avoid making a decision. But finally one weekend it all came crashing down and Gary had to get off the fence.

The trouble began when he received a long-distance call in his dorm room on Wednesday evening. "I've got a surprise," Janet chirped. "I've found a ride to the college this weekend."

"Yeah," Gary responded, trying to sound enthusiastic. But even while he was trying to figure out how to extricate himself from the pit he was in, the phone rang again, and this time it was Becky from across campus.

"Gary," she cooed, "I have some great news. You know that I've been wanting to introduce you to some members of my family. Well, this weekend is the time. They're coming to campus."

Uh-oh, Gary thought. The pit he was in had become a virtual Grand Canyon. It was threatening to swallow him whole. He tried to explain to Becky that an old friend was coming up for the weekend and he would have to be with her just on Friday evening to "clear up a misunderstanding." Becky would need to understand just this one time. She wasn't very happy, but what choice did she have?

42

Get Off the Fence

Friday evening arrived, all too quickly from Gary's perspective. The phone in his room rang. Janet had just arrived on campus and was already dressed for vespers. Gary knew he needed to take a walk with Janet, to tell her of his new friendship, but squirming at the thought, he headed for the dorm lobby, gave her a big hug, and headed off for vespers. In other words, he kept sitting on the fence.

Meanwhile, Becky's parents and sister had arrived on campus. Though they were disappointed not to meet her new boyfriend that night, she assured them they would do so the next day. Since they were running behind time for the vespers service, they sat in the church balcony. Hardly had they settled in their pew, though, than Becky looked down in the congregation below and saw Gary.

"Hey," she whispered proudly to her parents and sister. "See that handsome guy at the end of the second pew there? That's my new boyfriend."

However, as Mom, Dad, and Sis craned their necks to see her new beau, Becky focused her vision a little more closely on Gary. To her horror, she noticed that he was sitting quite close to another young lady. In fact, not only were they sitting close, they were holding hands tenderly. Janet had missed Gary a great deal and was eager for this chance for a little closeness. The unexpected sight did not escape the notice of Becky's family either. "Are you sure that is your boyfriend?" they asked. "If that is your boyfriend, then who is that he is sitting with?"

That night, after Gary returned to his room, the phone rang. It was Becky on the line, and she had a pointed message for Gary. There was no exchange of pleasantries. Her message was clear and unequivocal. It had a sharp edge. "Gary, you've got to make up your mind," she said. "Get off the fence!"

The pointed message with which she challenged him is relevant to each of God's children today: Get off the fence! Spiritually speaking, many people are straddling the fence. So many of us want to have it both ways. We want to know God, we want to go to heaven, but we also continue to cling to certain things that are detrimental to our Christian lives, things that lead us away from Jesus Christ.

Yes, lots of people are on the fence. To be totally honest, there is a fence sitter within each of us. The last of Revelation's seven churches, symbolizing the church of the last days, is the Laodicean church. The indictment of this church reads, " 'You are neither cold nor hot. I wish that you were either cold or hot. So, because you are lukewarm, and neither cold nor hot, I am about to spit you out of my mouth' " (Revelation 3:15, 16). One of the problems of the last-day church is sitting on the fence. But 1 Kings 18, the biblical passage under consideration in this chapter, challenges God's people to get off the fence and down on their knees.

Spiritually speaking, people were sitting on the fence in the days of Elijah. To use the biblical expression, they were " 'limping with two different opinions' " (1 Kings 18:21). Yes, it is true that some of the people of the Northern Kingdom of Israel worshiped Yahweh. But in an effort to assure the fertility of their land, they also worshiped Baal, the god of storms and rain. This was an untenable situation, for Yahweh demanded sole allegiance, undivided affection.

To bring matters to a head, Elijah went before King Ahab and announced, " 'As the Lord the God of Israel lives, before whom I stand, there shall be neither dew nor rain these years, except by my word' " (1 Kings 17:1). And thus it was, for more than three years. A terrible drought gripped the land. Crops withered. The ground was parched and cracked, devoid of moisture.

And it was not only the ground that was dry. Spiritually, the lives of the people were arid and dry. We can be certain of this, because sitting on the fence spiritually leaves you parched and thirsty, just like Death Valley.

Finally, when he thought he might at last gain some type of a hearing, Elijah appeared to Ahab and issued him a challenge: " 'Now therefore have all Israel assemble for me at Mount Carmel with the four hundred fifty prophets of Baal and the four hundred prophets of Asherah, who eat at Jezebel's table' " (1 Kings 18:19). Ahab accepted the challenge and gathered the people and the false prophets to Carmel, and the showdown was at hand.

There before the assembled group on Carmel, Elijah, though badly outnumbered, stepped forward and said to the people, " 'How long will you sit on the fence? If the Lord is God, follow him; but if Baal, then follow him.' Not a word did they answer" (1 Kings 18:21, NEB).

This question of Elijah echoes down through the centuries and it reverberates in the mind of each Christian today: How long will you sit on the fence? I have suggested that all of us are fence straddlers in some respects. It might be worth noting that fence sitters come in several varieties.

First, there are people who are "chameleons" in the way of their habits and lifestyle. They take on whatever characteristics make them fit in comfortably with the surrounding environment or with their peers. They blend in wherever they are. They are equally comfortable at a place of worship or at a place of entertainment that has no redeeming value. They can hear a sermon that speaks of Jesus' purity but then cut loose with a dirty joke or a little profanity now and then just to show they're not too holy. Chameleons are one variety of fence sitters.

Second, there are people who say they love Jesus, that they want to know Him, but aren't taking any time to make this happen. I remember when I first began dating the one whom I would later marry. I was so happy she had come into my life. I tried to spend as much time with her as I possibly could. I would show up at the hospital where she worked for her supper break. Later, when we had a long-distance relationship with an East Coast–West Coast time difference, we made numerous, lengthy phone calls in the middle of the night. Then there were the times I would take late-night flights as a courier. It all had a simple explanation. I was doing anything I could to spend time with her, to get to know her.

Sometimes we encourage people to try a devotional life as if that were an option, just like as a Southerner I might encourage people to sample grits or fried okra. Or on other occasions we tell people to "squeeze in a little time for Jesus," and we say it almost as if they are doing Him a favor. What audacity we have, encouraging people to "squeeze in a little time" for the Lord of the universe.

The truth of the matter is, if one wants growth in a relationship with Jesus it is indispensable to spend time with Him on a regular basis. That is one of the reasons the Sabbath is so important. God asks us to refrain from activities connected with our secular work and play for our own good. It is because these activities will diminish the growth that will take place in our relationship with Him on His day.

Third, there are individuals who claim to be Christians, but their actions are in stark contrast to that claim. In other words, their behavior contradicts their profession.

This is a good time to say something about the role of works or fruits in the Christian's life. One of the purposes of works is to serve as visible testimony to others that Jesus is Lord of our lives. While 1 Samuel 16:7 affirms that the Lord looks on the heart, it also states that humans look on the outward appearance. And because they do look on the outward appearance, when our lives display the Christians fruits, the fruits of the Spirit, it reveals that Jesus is alive in our hearts.

I am going to be rather specific now, so you might need to fasten your seat belt. It is deeply disturbing when God's special people who have advanced light on matters of health and understand that their bodies are temples of the Holy Spirit see no problem with the moderate use of alcohol. It is a cause for profound concern when professed Christians read Jesus' Sermon on the Mount and hear His clarion call to moral purity and then spend time delving into pornography. It is a cause of alarm when people who know the biblical teaching about the Sabbath sacrifice their appointment with God for employment that offers greater prosperity. It is troubling when the people of God read the counsel of Paul in Philippians 4:8 and then choose to rent videos that are not true, honorable, just, and pure.

Now don't misunderstand the point I am making here. It is true that Jesus loves us just the way we are. The Bible emphasizes this clearly, over and over again. But it is also true that He doesn't want us to stay that way. He wants to change us, to shape us, to mold us into His likeness. If Jesus is really your Savior, He will also be your Lord. Someone said it this way, "Jesus is either Lord of all, or He isn't Lord at all."

To illustrate, you might say our actions are like our uniform. Suppose it was just about time for the Super Bowl to begin and the coach of one team looked out on the field and saw his star quarterback wearing the uniform and helmet of the other team. He might rush out on the field and ask, "What's going on?" And his quarterback might reply, "Hey, coach, don't get bent out of shape about my outfit. I know in my heart I'm on your team. My appearance doesn't matter." And the coach would respond, "Of course it matters. What's the big idea? Whose side are you on anyway?"

And that is the question we face. Whose side are we on in the great controversy? When we claim to be followers of Jesus, but our actions belie that claim, we are straddling the fence.

Now there is some good news to the story of 1 Kings 18 for fence sitters. They should not be devoid of hope. The Bible indicates what to do. The simple solution is "Get off. Get off the fence, and get onto your knees."

"Then Elijah said to the people, 'I, even I only, am left a prophet of the Lord; but Baal's prophets number four hundred fifty. Let two bulls be given to us; let them choose one bull for themselves, cut it in pieces, and lay it on the wood, but put no fire to it; I will prepare the other bull and lay it on the wood, but put no fire to it. Then you call on the name of your god and I will call on the name of the Lord; the god who an-

swers by fire is indeed God.' All the people answered, 'Well spoken!' "
(1 Kings 18:22-24).

The prophets of Baal prepared their altar. They called on their
god. They shrieked and shouted, twisted and gyrated. But nothing
happened.

So Elijah decided to have a little fun. "At noon Elijah mocked them,
saying, 'Cry aloud! Surely he is a god; either he is meditating, or he has
wandered away, or he is on a journey, or perhaps he is asleep and must
be awakened.' Then they cried aloud and, as was their custom, they cut
themselves with swords and lances until the blood gushed out over them.
As midday passed, they raved on until the time of the offering of the
oblation, but there was no voice, no answer, and no response" (1 Kings
18:27-29).

In other words, Elijah taunted them. "What's wrong? Is your god
on vacation? Maybe he is going to the bathroom" (which is the possible
meaning of one of the Hebrew expressions). In reply, the prophets of
Baal jumped up and down, they cut themselves till the blood flowed in
order to garner the attention of their god, but in response there was
nothing but silence. There's a lesson in this: If we call on any god other
than the true God, we will receive no answer in our time of need. We
will be left alone in our anguish.

Finally, it was Elijah's turn. According to the Bible, he fixed up the
altar of Yahweh. He prepared the bull. Then he commanded that the
altar and the bull be drenched with gallons and gallons of water. Three
times they poured buckets over the sacrifice and the altar until they
were soaked.

Finally, the moment of drama arrived. "At the time of the offering
of the oblation, the prophet Elijah came near and said, 'O LORD, God
of Abraham, Isaac, and Israel, let it be known this day that you are God
in Israel, that I am your servant, and that I have done all these things at
your bidding. Answer me, O LORD, answer me, so that this people may
know that you, O LORD, are God, and that you have turned their hearts
back' " (1 Kings 18:36, 37).

It was a simple prayer. There were no wild gyrations. No special chants or magic incantations. Just a direct and uncluttered request to God. And what happened in reply?

"Then the fire of the LORD fell and consumed the burnt offering, the wood, the stones, and the dust, and even licked up the water that was in the trench. When all the people saw it, they fell on their faces and said, 'The LORD indeed is God; the LORD indeed is God'" (1 Kings 18:38, 39).

In other words, one can say that the people of Israel got off the fence and down on their knees. No longer were they fence sitters, no longer were they people who wanted to have it both ways, who couldn't make up their minds. They were off the fence and down on their knees.

It is very significant to notice what happened in the rest of 1 Kings 18. The drought came to an end, and God's rain began to fall (see 1 Kings 18:45). Not just a sprinkle or a shower. There was a downpour! No longer was the land parched and dry and cracked. Rain, sweet rain, was falling.

What happened long ago in Israel is symbolic of what God wants to do for each of us individually and for His church corporately. If we get off the fence, if we let go of the things that are separating us from Jesus, His blessings will shower our lives. And corporately, as a church family, if we climb down from the fence and get onto our knees, the rain of revival will fall in our midst. No longer will our church services be arid and dry. God's blessing can fall—it will fall.

There is one more point to make. It might seem scary to clamber off the fence because of the change it will bring. But it is worth emphasizing that when we get off the fence we aren't going down into an abyss, we aren't falling into a dark canyon. In fact, Someone is waiting for us there.

One Sabbath afternoon my family was out for a walk. Unexpectedly, a four-foot tall fence loomed in our path. It seemed as though we were at an impasse. What could we do? We didn't want to go back, but going forward was difficult. My wife and I could climb over the fence, but it wasn't so easy for our two boys.

Finally, we came up with an idea. I would go over the fence first and help the rest of the family over. My wife, Mary, would help our boys up the fence on the other side. It seemed like a workable plan.

Our youngest son, Joshua, just a small tyke then, was OK with the idea, at least until he made it up to the top of the fence. But while perched on the top, he got worried. His situation looked so precarious to him, so scary. He got an anxious expression on his little face.

So I extended my arms toward him, and when he saw his father's extended arms, a smile creased his face. He quickly came down on my side of the fence. He knew it would be OK, because he was going into his father's arms.

As you climb off the fence, look to Jesus. His arms are open. He is waiting there to receive you.

CHAPTER 6

When You Hit Rock Bottom

1 Kings 19:1-18

Here is a riddle: Name a place that everyone has been to but to which no one wants to return. Now you might need to scratch your head and think for a while. Some people who prefer sunshine and high temperatures might propose one of the northern states as the answer to this question, but that would not be correct. They would simply be showing their bias for warm weather, and additionally, not everyone has traveled to the north. My wife, who grew up in California where the humidity is usually quite low, might propose one of the southeastern United States where the summertime air is often sultry and moisture-laden. However, some people prefer the South to other regions, and a number of people have never been there, so that rules out the South as a correct answer. Actually, it is nearly impossible to find a place to which everyone has been but to which no one wants to return. However, there is one such place. It is called Rock Bottom.

The phrase *rock bottom* means "the lowest point" or "as low as it can get," so it is a good metaphor for a time of discouragement. "Hitting rock bottom" is a good expression to denote a time of despair. It is a fitting term for a time when someone has no idea where to turn. It is a good way to describe a period when someone is depressed, downcast, and ready to give up. Rock Bottom—you know about that place. So do I.

Rock Bottom is where you are when your emotional strength is gone and you are completely drained. Rock Bottom is where you are when your support group has dwindled away and there is no one to lean on. Rock Bottom is where you are when you wonder if life is worth living, whether there is any reason to keep going. Rock Bottom is where you are when your spiritual experience seems nonexistent and you feel as though your prayers are falling to the earth instead of winging their way towards heaven. And perhaps that is the worst thing of all about Rock Bottom. Not only do we feel deserted by others, we sometimes feel abandoned by the Lord also.

Rock Bottom—you know all about that place, don't you? You've been there before. And you have no desire to go back!

Maybe you hit Rock Bottom shortly after you joined the church. On the day of your conversion or your baptism, when you asked Jesus into your heart, you thought that everything would go smoothly, that you would live "happily ever after" as part of a loving church family that got along perfectly. However, your spiritual high crashed into reality as you discovered that the other church members weren't quite perfect yet, and to be honest, neither were you.

Maybe you landed at Rock Bottom shortly after painful divorce proceedings, when the rest of the church treated you like a leper, as though you had a communicable disease, and they kept their distance. Perhaps you found yourself at Rock Bottom following the death of a loved one, after the flowers had faded and the members of your support group had returned to their busy lives and you were left alone with so many painful memories and vexing questions.

Rock Bottom—you know more than you care to know about that place. You've been to that place. In fact, maybe you are there right now, this very moment. As you read this book, you are hoping for something or someone to lift you out of the pit of discouragement in which you find yourself.

One of the challenges faced by the inhabitants of Rock Bottom is that they don't receive much support or encouragement. Other people don't always understand. Some well-meaning people will try to help by mouthing platitudes like, "Well, when things are this bad, they can't get any worse." And you feel like replying sarcastically, "Thanks, that's just the encouragement I needed." To tell someone who is at Rock Bottom that it can't get any worse is like telling a person who is drowning in twenty feet of water that the pond doesn't get any deeper. That news doesn't offer much comfort or hope. No, platitudes don't help you when you hit rock bottom.

Sometimes Rock Bottom dwellers are eager to tell their plight to other people, but the other people are not eager to hear. While at church or at work, they may hear the question, "How are you doing?" but before they have an opportunity to respond the person who asked is hastening on their way.

Rock Bottom—it's not a pleasant place to be. However, since all of us are there at some time or other, a relevant question is this: How should we handle it when we are at Rock Bottom? In other words, when we hit Rock Bottom, what should we do?

To answer that question, let's examine a Rock Bottom experience in the life of the prophet Elijah, an experience that is often overlooked. From the outset it is helpful to know that God's most faithful men and women of old sometimes hit Rock Bottom, and God did not forsake them. Far from it! In fact, He was right there with them, being especially close when they were at Rock Bottom.

As 1 Kings 19 begins, Elijah had just experienced a day that most preachers only dream of. Fire from heaven had descended in answer to his prayer and had consumed a sacrifice dripping with water, and all the people had bowed to the ground proclaiming Yahweh to be the true God. Then Elijah had prayed again, this time seven times, and showers of rain had drenched the parched, thirsty earth.

And now, after leading Ahab's chariot back to the palace at Jezreel, he waited for a message. He wanted to see what King Ahab and Queen Jezebel would say about the events of the day. After such spectacular events on Mt. Carmel, he was exceedingly hopeful. Perhaps Ahab and Jezebel would declare an end to all Baal worship and ask him to lead out in the reform. Possibly the king and queen themselves would now worship the true God. They might even make him an official prophet of the court and give him a place to live in the palace, with a generous stipend to boot. Surely the messenger would come with good news. Following the fireworks on Carmel, how could anyone dispute the supremacy of the true God?

How crestfallen, how bitterly disappointed Elijah must have been to hear the following words from Jezebel: " 'So may the gods do to me, and more also, if I do not make your life like the life of one of them by this time tomorrow' " (1 Kings 19:2). In other words, she was threatening to execute him just as he had done to the prophets of Baal.

Perhaps Elijah paused for a moment in disbelief, with thoughts like these racing through his mind. *After the great victory on Carmel, nothing has changed. Jezebel is just the same, just as evil as ever. She's still the queen. And where are all the people who fell on their faces when the fire of God descended from heaven and consumed the sacrifice? Where are they? And where is God? He is the One who got me into all this mess anyway.*

At first glance it seems hard to believe what happens next to this man who was so brave and unflinching on Mt. Carmel, who faced off with and defeated 450 prophets of Baal, who stood alone for God. It seems hard to believe, but it is true. At the threat of one angry woman Elijah took off in terror, frantically fleeing for his life, running pell-mell, helter-skelter, as fast as he could go. On and on he went, some one hundred miles on foot into the Judean desert. After leaving his servant at Beer-Sheba, he continued on alone until he finally found himself in a desolate wilderness, where he sat down under a small tree.

Once he was there, the real trouble began. Depression set in. Despondency. Despair. He knew that he didn't belong there. He knew that God had not commanded him to flee. He was disappointed with the leaders of the nation, he was disappointed with others, but most of all, he was disappointed in himself. He had hit Rock Bottom. And in his utter discouragement, while there at Rock Bottom, "he asked that he might die: 'It is enough; now, O LORD, take away my life, for I am no better than my ancestors'" (1 Kings 19:4). This is the same Elijah who had stood toe to toe with an idolatrous king and several hundred false prophets, yet now he was praying that his own life might be brought to an end.

Have you ever noticed that often the highs and the lows of life are very close together? It is a geographical fact that Mount Whitney, the highest point in the contiguous forty-eight states, towering some 14,494 feet above the state of California, is less than a hundred miles from Death Valley, the lowest point in the same area, which sinks some 282 feet below sea level. And that is a metaphor of life, a reflection of human experience. Often our spiritual mountaintops, the times when all is going well, are closely followed by a slide into the valley of discouragement.

And while we may have a hard time knowing how Elijah felt on Mt. Carmel, and we might not be able to understand it fully, we can all identify with him when he hits Rock Bottom. Everyone knows how it feels to be discouraged, to be depressed, what it's like to feel like giving up.

Many times we have the confidence that God is with us when we are spiritually high, when we are atop our Mt. Carmel, but feel that He has left us alone when we hit Rock Bottom, when we suffer from discouragement and depression. Nothing could be further from the truth! We must notice this aspect of the experience of Elijah: God doesn't leave us alone to wallow in our discouragement. He doesn't forsake us when we hit Rock Bottom. He doesn't condemn us. He doesn't inquire, "What's your problem?" He doesn't just command,

"Get on your feet." Instead, His healing love works to heal our troubled hearts.

In this encounter with Elijah, God took four steps to heal the prophet's discouraged, troubled heart. Let us notice God's strategy, for it will assist us if we are at Rock Bottom now, or if we find ourselves there in the future.

The first step the Lord took is this. After Elijah prayed that he might die, God refreshed him physically. Look at 1 Kings 19:5-7: "Then he lay down under the broom tree and fell asleep. Suddenly an angel touched him and said to him, 'Get up and eat.' He looked, and there at his head was a cake baked on hot stones, and a jar of water. He ate and drank, and lay down again. The angel of the Lord came a second time, touched him, and said, 'Get up and eat, otherwise the journey will be too much for you.' "

God's first gift to take His child out of Rock Bottom was simply food and rest. Now sometimes we portray God as the type who would have reached down and yanked Elijah by the nape of the neck and said, "Get out of this wilderness! What do you mean by being so discouraged after all I have done for you? You're letting me down!" But there is something wonderfully gentle about the way the Lord treats His discouraged child, sending the angel to touch him lightly, giving him food, letting him rest some more, and then giving more food.

Of course, God knows what we many times forget. There is an integral connection between the physical and the spiritual. They cannot be separated from one another. Have you noticed how tired people—yourself included—are often cranky and irritable? Often when we are physically weak and emotionally exhausted, we are also spiritually discouraged. And sometimes when we are at Rock Bottom emotionally, what we need most of all is a good night's sleep and a nourishing meal.

Jesus had sent the disciples out two-by-two to share the message of His love and grace. When they returned, anxious to tell Him about their ministry of preaching and healing, eager to have some private time with Jesus, He invited them: " 'Come away to a deserted place all by yourselves and rest a while.' For many were coming and going, and they had no leisure even to eat" (Mark 6:31).

Now they could have responded, "But, Jesus, You Yourself said that 'the fields are ripe for harvesting' (John 4:35). We can't afford to take time off." However, Jesus knew what they needed most of all—rest and refreshment, physical and spiritual nourishment. Time with Him.

One time Jesus had been preaching to the multitude all day, and they were becoming hungry. Perhaps their stomachs were growling. Jesus was concerned about their physical need, and He worked a miracle to supply it (see Mark 6:30-44).

We are no different from Elijah, no different from the disciples. When we are discouraged or depressed, when we hit Rock Bottom, God says, "Have some food. Get some rest." He gives us physical refreshment.

There is a second step the Lord took to extricate Elijah from Rock Bottom. Simply stated, God spoke to His child. After God had supplied him with food and allowed him to rest, Elijah traveled on to Mt. Horeb (another name for Mt. Sinai). He found a cave, perhaps the very cleft of the rock where Moses had crouched many years before when God had caused His glory to pass by (see Exodus 33:22). As Elijah cowered in the cave in discouragement and shame, perhaps thinking he was all alone, the Bible states that "the word of the Lord came to him" (1 Kings 19:9).

I like the way Scripture expresses this concept, using an active verb ("came") to describe God speaking His message to Elijah. It is as if the Lord's word is active and moving and will seek you out, even if you are at Rock Bottom, even if you are hiding in discouragement and shame.

If truth be told, when you are at Rock Bottom, when you are depressed and you feel like giving up, when the loneliness is oppressive, what you need most of all is to hear the voice of God, the voice of the

One who cares about you more than anyone else. I think of Mary Magdalene standing outside the Garden Tomb that special day so many years ago. As she lingered there, she was discouraged and hopeless. There didn't seem to be any reason to go on living. But just this one word from the lips of her risen Lord—"Mary," He said (John 20:16)—and her whole world changed and her night turned to day.

The same is true for you. God doesn't leave you alone, for when you are at Rock Bottom, when hope seems gone, He speaks to you just as He did to Elijah and Mary.

It is instructive to notice how He spoke to Elijah. Not in the mighty wind, not through the earthquake, not in the fire (1 Kings 19:11). After these powerful displays, there was "a sound of sheer silence" (1 Kings 19:12), and then God communicated with His child.

That "still small voice," as the King James Version calls it, had a lesson for Elijah, and it has a lesson for you and me today. It is this: Every day with God will not be a Mt. Carmel experience. The Lord does not always come with a spectacular display of fireworks, with a great extravaganza. What we need as Christians today is not more blazing displays of divine power and majestic miracles. Rather, we need to hear that still, small voice of God speaking to us in personal Bible study, in our prayer lives. For those who are at Rock Bottom, the still, small voice calls out an invitation: " 'Come to me, all you that are weary and are carrying heavy burdens, and I will give you rest' " (Matt. 11:28).

The third step God took to pull Elijah out of Rock Bottom is that He gave Elijah a work to do. He gave him a task to fulfill. First Kings 19:15-17 tells how the Lord instructed Elijah to anoint Elisha and Jehu and Hazael. The Lord knew that one of the biggest reasons for Elijah's discouragement was that he thought his work as a prophet was finished. He felt that he had been an abject and utter failure and that he no longer deserved to work for God. So there he was, loitering in a cave out in the middle of nowhere, doing nothing. In essence the Lord said, "I still need you. I have a work for you to do."

The same is true when we hit Rock Bottom. When we are discouraged, we tend to sit on our hands, so to speak. We tend to minimize what talents we have, and we hide them under a bushel. Or we feel that the church does not need our abilities. In a sense, we, like Elijah, are cowering in the cave of our despondency and despair.

But we must remember that according to Scripture, the church is like a body, and if one part is missing or is not performing its function, the whole body suffers. A friend of mine provided a living illustration of this truth. He made the mistake of riding barefoot on his bicycle. Unfortunately for him, his toes got entangled with the chain and sprocket, and he came out minus one of his little toes. Now someone might think, one missing little toe shouldn't hamper a person from doing all that they did before. But when the soreness receded and he was able to walk again, he discovered that his walking was affected. He was thrown off balance. One of the smallest parts of the body was missing, and it impaired his ability to walk.

Even so, each part of the body of Christ is needed. Every member is important. When you hit Rock Bottom you must remember this: God needs you. He has a work for you to do.

The final step God took to heal Elijah's hurting heart was to remind him of something important he should remember. Once God had refreshed him physically, had spoken to him and commissioned him with a new work, the Lord reminded him of something he needed to know.

Elijah, in something of a self-serving comment, had expressed his opinion that he was the only one who was really committed to God. He was the only one who was "true-blue," or so he thought, the only one who was really faithful. " 'I have been very zealous for the Lord, the God of hosts; for the Israelites have forsaken your covenant, thrown down your altars, and killed your prophets with the sword. I alone am left, and they are seeking my life, to take it away,' " he declared (1 Kings 19:14).

In reply, God informed Elijah his numbers were way off. He said, " 'Yet I will leave seven thousand in Israel, all the knees that have not bowed to Baal, and every mouth that has not kissed him' " (1 Kings 19:18). God was letting Elijah know that he was wrong to think of himself in isolation. Far from being alone in his commitment to the Lord, there was a group of seven thousand that remained faithful to God.

Sometimes we are the same as Elijah. We see the rampant immorality and materialism in society, we see a lack of commitment in the church, and we think we are all alone in the great struggle against evil. But God still has His seven thousand, a group who are faithful to Him. Furthermore, numbers do not win the battle anyway, for when we are on God's side, victory is certain.

If you are at Rock Bottom, there is no need to stay there. God yearns to soothe your troubled soul. He wants to refresh you physically and to speak to you with His still, small voice. He will give you a task to do for Him and remind you that you aren't alone. When you hit Rock Bottom, there's no need to stay.

CHAPTER 7

Standing for God

2 Chronicles 18; 1 Kings 22

Several years ago I had the opportunity of visiting Yad Vashem, the museum of the Holocaust, during a trip to Israel. If you have been either to Yad Vashem or to its sister museum in Washington, D.C., you know what a memorable experience it is. Perhaps a haunting experience would be more precise. I took a poignant walk through the unforgettable Hall of Children, where a voice intones name after name of the young ones whose lives were cut short during this tragic era of history. I saw the starkness of the engraved stones commemorating all the Jews who were gassed in Dachau, Treblinka, Sobibor, Auschwitz, and the other houses of horror that Hitler's henchmen constructed. I viewed other reminders of this dark epoch in the twentieth century, which is painful to remember but that we must not forget.

If there was one positive note during my otherwise sad, reflective tour, it was my walk down the Avenue of the Righteous Gentiles. This walkway is surrounded by trees planted in honor of those non-Jews who worked to rescue Jews from the fate the Nazis had planned for them, sometimes at the cost of their own lives. Person after person is memorialized by a tree and by a plaque engraved with their names. These are people who stood for God and for right and for truth, often standing alone, often at great danger to themselves. For instance, John Weidner, the Seventh-day Adventist who almost forfeited his own life as the head of the Dutch-Paris underground and whose sister did die in Nazi hands, is remembered with a tree in his honor.

As I reflect on my time there, it strikes me that the men and women remembered on the Avenue of the Righteous Gentiles are the type of people called for and described in the following well-known quote: "The greatest want of the world is the want of men— men who will not be bought or sold, men who in their inmost souls are true and honest, men who do not fear to call sin by its right name, men whose conscience is true to duty as the needle to the pole, men who will stand for the right though the heavens fall" (*Education*, 57).

This quote and my time at Yad Vashem cause me to ask some questions: Do I have the moral courage of John Weidner or the Ten Boom family (the Dutch watchmakers described in the book *The Hiding Place,* who rescued Jews at the cost of the lives of several family members)? Would I be willing to risk my life in order to do what was right, to stand up for what was good and true? Am I brave enough to stand alone if necessary, as God's children have needed to do again and again down through history? What does it take to stand up for God anyway?

The biblical story under consideration in this chapter highlights one man who had just this type of courage. He had what it took to stand up for God. He was a man who stood up for truth to a wicked, idolatrous king of Israel and a well-meaning but vacillating king of Judah, a man who bore witness to a secular messenger of the king and who faced down four hundred false prophets. He was a man who knew what it meant to stand alone. Though not as well known as his esteemed contemporaries Elijah and Elisha, Micaiah-ben Imlah deserves to be recognized as their equal in courage and commitment. He deserves to be viewed as a model of what it means to stand for God. To his story we now turn.

Jehoshaphat, the king of Judah, had come on a state visit to see Ahab, king of Israel. Now Jehoshaphat was an intriguing and paradoxical character. On the one hand, he was notable for his spiritual achievements and commitment to Yahweh. As the Bible states, "The Lord was with Jehoshaphat, because he walked in the earlier ways of his father; he did not seek the Baals, but sought the God of his father and walked in his commandments, and not according to the ways of Israel. Therefore the Lord established the kingdom in his hand. All Judah brought tribute to Jehoshaphat, and he had great riches and honor. His heart was courageous in the ways of the Lord; and furthermore he removed the high places and the sacred poles from Judah" (2 Chronicles 17:3-6).

On the other hand, he apparently had no scruples about forming a marriage alliance with one of the most wicked royal families in the entire history of the monarchy, giving his son Jehoram to be the husband of Athaliah, daughter of Ahab and Jezebel (see 2 Chronicles 21:6). Additionally, in the story under consideration in this chapter, he was willing to unite his armies with Ahab to fight a common enemy (see 2 Chronicles 18), and he later joined with the wicked Ahaziah in an ill-fated trading expedition (see 2 Chronicles 20:35-37).

While Jehoshaphat was on this state visit, Ahab decided to use the opportunity to do some military planning. The city of Ramoth-gilead, located on the eastern side of the Jordan, was controlled by the armies of Aram (Syria), and Ahab was not satisfied with the situation. Ramoth-gilead was within the borders that had been originally granted to Israel, and Ahab felt it should be returned to Israelite hands, even if it took force to do so.

Knowing that the Israelite forces would be strengthened by the addition of Judah's army, Ahab inquired whether Jehoshaphat would be willing to join in the attempt to retake Ramoth-gilead. Jehoshaphat answered, " 'I am with you, my people are your people. We will be with you in the war' " (2 Chronicles 18:3). In other words, Jehoshaphat said, "We're in this together. You can count on the army of Judah to fight right beside you."

But then something interesting happened. Almost as if pricked by his conscience for answering without first consulting God or praying for divine wisdom, he added a request: "But Jehoshaphat also said to the king of Israel, 'Inquire first for the word of the Lord' " (2 Chronicles 18:4). While this was a noble-sounding request, it was a bit late in light of the fact that Jehoshaphat had already offered his complete support and his own army to Ahab. It was no longer possible to "inquire first" of the Lord's word since Jehoshaphat had already pledged his complete support. Perhaps he recognized that he had gotten the cart in front of the horse.

To comply with Jehoshaphat's request, Ahab called in the prophets, 400 in number (see 2 Chronicles 18:5; notice the similarity in number with the 450 prophets of Baal and the 400 prophets of Asherah mentioned in the Mt. Carmel narrative; see 1 Kings 18:19). There is no indication in the text that it required great effort or took a lot of time to get these prophets together. It is likely that these men were what could be called "court prophets." They worked for the king and were on his payroll. This is not an insignificant matter, because as the story demonstrates, they knew where their bread was buttered. They knew to whom they owed allegiance. The one who paid the piper, namely, Ahab, called the tune.

King Ahab posed the question at hand to them: " 'Shall we go to battle against Ramoth-gilead, or shall I refrain?' They said, 'Go up; for God will give it into the hand of the king' " (2 Chronicles 18:5). Of course this is what they said! They knew what the king wanted to hear, so they chose to make him happy. You might say that each one stuck a finger in the air to see which way the wind of royal preference was blowing, and they went with the direction of the wind.

But there was something about the way the issue was handled that made Jehoshaphat uncomfortable and nervous. Though he had answered Ahab's inquiry very quickly and with no careful consideration (see 2 Chronicles 18:3), it bothered him when these prophets did the same. Perhaps in the answer of the prophets he recognized the problems with his own reply. These 400 prophets seemed too much like sycophants, trying to win the favor of the king by flattering him. Maybe he realized that anytime 400 clergy agree on anything, you'd better watch out!

In any case, he was not satisfied with what he had seen and heard. He was not yet satisfied that he had a divine go-ahead for the war against Aram. In an implicit criticism of both the prophets that had spoken thus far and Ahab who had paraded them in, Jehoshaphat said to Ahab, " 'Is there no other prophet of the Lord here of whom we may inquire?' " (2 Chronicles 18:6). Yes, indicated Ahab, there is one such man named Micaiah, " 'but I hate him, for he never prophesies anything favorable about me, but only disaster' " (2 Chronicles 18:7).

A messenger was sent to fetch Micaiah. While the two monarchs waited for his arrival, the 400 prophets began livening up the festivities with a pep rally to strengthen and underscore their declaration that Ahab should proceed to attack Ramoth-gilead. Zedekiah, their ringleader, even took a set of iron horns and placed them on his head to illustrate the point. "He said, 'Thus says the Lord: With these you shall gore the Arameans until they are destroyed' " (2 Chronicles 18:10). And Zedekiah was not alone, for "all the prophets were prophesying the same thing and saying: 'Go up to Ramoth-gilead and triumph; the Lord will give it into the hand of the king' " (2 Chronicles 18:11).

Picture the scene. Two kings clothed in royal robes, sitting on thrones at the entrance of the Israelite capital of Samaria, surrounded by a group of cheering, shouting yes-men who are telling King Ahab just what he wants to hear. Talk about pressure to conform! Talk about being under duress! It would be difficult to think of a more challenging situation for one to step into and utter a note contrary to what was being said. It would be hard to imagine a scenario requiring more courage than this one for someone to stand up and be different.

The pressure to conform was made even worse by the messenger who went to summon Micaiah. This nameless individual left his mark in the biblical record by encouraging Micaiah to sing in harmony with the group of prophets who had already spoken to the king. He said, " 'Look, the words of the prophets with one accord are favorable to the king; let your word be like the word of one of them, and speak favorably' " (2 Chronicles 18:12). Reading between the lines, the messenger was saying something like this: "Hey, buddy, it's no skin off my back, but do yourself a favor this one time. Don't rock the boat. All the other prophets are telling the king what he wants to hear. Just this one time, you should do the same."

But Micaiah's primary concern was not about how he would be treated. Rather, his interest was in being faithful to God and standing up for Him. In those never-to-be-forgotten words that were the hallmark of the prophetic office, he said, " 'As the Lord lives, whatever my God says, that I will speak' " (2 Chronicles 18:13).

Self-interest, self-preservation, self-promotion—all of these were important for the court prophets, but not to the true man of God. He was willing to stand for truth, even if it meant standing alone. Being faithful to the Lord was his primary concern.

Oddly enough, after his bold declaration that he must speak only the truth in Yahweh's name, Micaiah seems at first glance to have contradicted his own statement. When he was asked whether the kings should proceed with their military plans, he replied, " 'Go up and triumph; they will be given into your hand' " (2 Chronicles 18:14). How should this statement be understood? Perhaps Micaiah was speaking ironically or even sarcastically. Perhaps he was implying, "Go ahead. This is what your own prophets are telling you. Why do you need me?"

Whatever the meaning of Micaiah's initial statement, it is clear that Ahab was suspicious of what Micaiah had said, so he issued a verbal challenge. "But the king said to him, 'How many times must I make you swear to tell me nothing but the truth in the name of the Lord?' Then Micaiah said, 'I saw all Israel scattered on the mountains, like sheep without a shepherd; and the Lord said, "These have no master; let each one go home in peace" ' " (2 Chronicles 18:15, 16). In other words, through his prophetic eye Micaiah envisioned the upcoming battle and heard the divine pronouncement that Israel no longer had a leader and that the Israelite soldiers should return home.

Though the encounter at the city gate continued a little longer and included a description by Micaiah of a strange scene at the heavenly court (see 2 Chronicles 18:18-22) and intense verbal sparring between Micaiah and the leader of the false prophets (see 2 Chronicles 18:23, 24), for Ahab the gauntlet had already been thrown down. His pride affronted, he probably felt that he could not back down from the challenge of Micaiah. He had to go to war with Aram or he would lose face. He had to rise to the challenge.

He did by throwing his own gauntlet to the ground. Notwithstanding the fact that in proclaiming the prophetic word Micaiah was simply doing what Ahab had commanded him to do (see 2 Chronicles 18:15), Ahab felt that Micaiah should pay a penalty for his impudence. Turn him over to the custody of my son, Ahab ordered, and " ' "put this fellow in prison and feed him on reduced rations of bread and water until I return in peace" ' " (2 Chronicles 18:26). The last part of this statement was especially significant. "Until I return in peace" meant that, whatever Micaiah may have said about Israel having no leader, don't believe it. Ahab will return.

But Micaiah threw the gauntlet right back: " 'If you return in peace, the Lord has not spoken by me.' " And to make sure his words were not forgotten and to call the onlookers to pay attention to the contest and watch for its outcome, he added, " 'Hear, you peoples, all of you!' " (2 Chronicles 18:27).

In due time, the armies of Israel and Judah, led by their kings, sallied forth to battle against Ramoth-gilead. Of course, from the biblical perspective, their defeat was only to be expected. They were going against the word of the Lord, and that always places one on dangerous ground. Evidently, Ahab had a premonition that something bad would happen to him personally (did he believe Micaiah after all?), so he disguised himself as a common soldier (see 2 Chronicles 18:29). But his disguise was to no avail, and the story moves toward its expected denouement.

"A certain man drew his bow and unknowingly struck the king of Israel between the scale armor and the breastplate" (2 Chronicles 18:33). No disguise was able to protect him from the Lord's arrow of retribution. The wound was a fatal one and led to an ignominious end for the king; for "they washed the chariot by the pool of Samaria; the dogs licked up his blood, and the prostitutes washed themselves in it" (1 Kings 22:38).

It is instructive and worthwhile to review the various leading characters involved in this story we have looked at in this chapter. Though the actors in the drama are long dead, their various personalities are still with us. To be more accurate, *we are* these personalities.

First, there is Jehoshaphat. Jehoshaphat wanted to do right. He had good intentions. He even prodded King Ahab to seek out a prophet of the Lord, to get a second opinion as to whether the battle plans were in accordance with God's will. But in the final analysis, he comes off none too positively, because when all is said and done he is willing to compromise truth. At the end of the day, he is known in 2 Chronicles 18, not for standing for truth but for sitting down with falsehood in the person of Ahab. He only makes a brief appearance in the battle itself and that is to cry out in fear of his life (2 Chronicles 18:31). This is hardly a profile in courage.

Then there is Zedekiah, the leader of the false prophets. This is the man who put on the iron horns to symbolize the strength and vigor he stated God would give to Israel in order to vanquish its enemies. He slapped Micaiah, God's true prophet, on the cheek and mocked him sarcastically (2 Chronicles 18:23). After doing so, he received a prediction from the prophet that was a portent of peril (2 Chronicles 18:24). Though he was clearly on the wrong side of the equation from the divine perspective, one thing can be said for him: It is clear which side he was on. He was not lukewarm and neither hot nor cold. Unlike Jehoshaphat, who drifted and vacillated, Zedekiah put down his stakes and took a position.

Then there is the messenger who advised Micaiah to agree with the other prophets. He didn't feel it necessary to take a position on what was right or wrong. He simply wanted to encourage Micaiah to do himself a favor by going along with the other prophets. This man serves as a good symbol of the average secular person who simply doesn't want to get involved, who doesn't want to take a stand one way or the other. This type of person will simply encourage God's children to act out of self-interest, which is not to be our primary concern.

Next comes Ahab. Ahab was in some respects the mirror image of Jehoshaphat, but on the wrong side of the equation. Though a wicked, idolatrous king, he had Jehoshaphat as a friend. In this case he was even willing to consult a true prophet of the Lord—but not to follow what he counseled. There seems to be some little part of him that was not totally given over to evil. But in the end that part was dominated and overwhelmed by the rest of Ahab when he disregarded the divine warning. In light of this, one would expect Ahab to meet with no other end than the inglorious one with which he met.

Finally, there is Micaiah. By his moral courage and dedication to God he demonstrated what it takes to stand for God. What did it take anyway? And more important, what does it take now? That is, what characteristics and qualities are required in one who would stand for God today?

The following qualities are highlighted in this story. First, standing for God requires standing against evil. It means to oppose moral wickedness in the world. Certainly this was the case with Micaiah. When Ahab first thought of him as a possible way to hear a word from God, he responded strongly, " 'I hate him' " (2 Chronicles 18:7). Clearly, Ahab was not neutral toward Micaiah, and the reason is that Micaiah was not neutral toward Ahab's wickedness.

This raises a question for God's children today. Have we adopted the stance of Micaiah? Do we stand for the Lord by standing against evil? Are we willing to oppose the moral wickedness that abounds in society today, whether it be a wanton disregard of human life as witnessed in the startlingly high numbers of abortions and cases of infanticide or the permissiveness towards pornography and adultery, evils which wreak such havoc in American families? Or are we in danger of assimilating the values of the culture in which we live?

If we are tempted just to go with the flow, to go along and get along so we won't stir things up, to compromise with evil, we must remember the example of Micaiah and Jehoshaphat. While the former is remembered as standing for the Lord, straight and true, like a sturdy oak, the latter is recalled as a timid, vacillating monarch whose legacy is marred by his compromise with evil (see 2 Chronicles 20:35-37). Their example underscores the following truth: To stand for God means to oppose evil.

Second, standing for God means adopting God's agenda, fulfilling the divine plan for one's life, regardless of the consequences. When Micaiah was challenged to endorse Ahab's military agenda and make it easier for himself by telling the king what he wanted to hear, his response was crystal clear: " 'As the Lord lives, whatever my God says, that I will speak' " (2 Chronicles 18:13).

What about us today? Is our agenda to live in harmony with the plan that God has for us? Can each of us honestly say to ourselves, "Today, right now, I will do what God has for me to do, speak the words He has for me to say, touch the lives He has for me to touch. Is it my greatest desire to fulfill the plan the Lord has for me?"

Perhaps one of the greatest temptations Christians face today is to do God's will and accomplish His plan on the occasions that it benefits us and then claim that we are standing for Him. While some may be fooled by such conduct and others may even applaud it, God is not deceived. Even in our own heart of hearts we know the truth. This is not standing for God; it is only serving our own interests.

As Micaiah demonstrated, to stand for God means to speak the words and do the works that God would have us do. It means that our greatest desire in life is to do God's will. It means that we join Jesus in saying, " 'My food is to do the will of Him who sent me and to complete His work' " (John 4:34).

Finally, standing for God means being willing to stand alone. It means to be outnumbered, to be in the minority. It means to have little in the way of human support. Micaiah received precious little encouragement in this story. Jehoshaphat, the king who suggested he be consulted, said nothing while Micaiah was being verbally abused and slapped about. In fact, once Micaiah had been summoned, there is no mention of Jehoshaphat making a peep until he cried out in fear of his own life (see 2 Chronicles 18:31). Certainly Micaiah received no support from Ahab or Zedekiah, the leader of the false prophets.

What took place that day simply emphasizes a truth that has been demonstrated time and again down through history, namely, to stand for God often means standing alone. It was true for Elijah on Mt. Carmel (see 1 Kings 18). It was true for Stephen as he stood before the Sanhedrin (see Acts 6, 7). It was true for Jesus in Pilate's judgment hall (see John 18). And it is just as true today.

But to truly understand what it means to stand for God, something else should be noted. As he stood tall for God that day so long ago, Micaiah had two things that no one else had. First, he had the compelling power of truth on his side. While Ahab was apprehensive about the course of action he chose, disguising himself in battle (see 2 Chronicles 18:29), and while Jehoshaphat was in fear of his life (see 2 Chronicles 18:31), we see no fear or self-doubt with Micaiah. He was supremely confident, bold and unflinching, because truth was on his side. The power of truth is a mighty force propelling those who stand for God to accomplish great things for Him. It provides inner strength and fortitude, enabling God's people to stand for Him even when the world is arrayed against them. Even when they are alone.

The second thing Micaiah had involves modifying the above point. Not only was truth on his side, he also had the presence of God. So while humanly speaking he may have been alone, in reality he was not alone. The Lord who promises "I am with you always" (see Matthew 28:20) stood with His faithful servant in that hostile encounter with Ahab and his false prophets.

We might state it this way: To stand for God means to stand with God. He never abandons those who stand for Him. Just as He was with Joseph in his trials and tribulations (see Gen. 39:21, 23), so He is with His children today. Whatever their situation, even when they walk through the valley of the shadow of death, those who stand alone for God are not really alone.

Interestingly enough, we do not know what became of Micaiah. He is never mentioned in the Bible after this story. The last picture we have is the snapshot of him being led away to prison with the command to feed him a bare minimum. However, what we do know is that we need not worry about him. Though he stood alone for God, ultimately he was not alone. God stood with him then, and will do so throughout eternity. And thus it will be for all who stand up for God.

CHAPTER 8

Listening to His Voice

1 Kings 19:19-21

The hot sun blistered down on the young man plowing the field. He stopped to wipe the perspiration from his brow for the hundredth time and looked around the field, wishing that he were finished with his work so he could go inside and find some respite from the heat. He was not done though, and since there was no shade in the field, he decided he might as well continue and finish as quickly as possible.

As he turned back to his plowing, an odd thing happened. A man with distinctive appearance and dress (see 2 Kings 1:8) came striding across the field, walked over to Elisha, wrapped his jacket around him, and started to continue on his way. Now Elisha could have responded in a variety of ways. He could have said, "No thanks, this jacket is the last thing I need. I'm hot enough as it is." He could have simply ignored the rather strange action. But instead, in Elijah's strange action he heard the voice of God, and equally important, he decided to respond to that voice.

As we examine these verses from 2 Kings 19:19-21, which depict the call of Elisha to the prophetic office, we discover two characteristics that are worthy of imitation today, two qualities that each of God's contemporary children should try to emulate. The first characteristic is that Elisha heard the voice of God.

73

As indicated above, it was a rather strange way to hear God's voice. As the Bible describes it, "So he [Elijah] set out from there, and found Elisha son of Shaphat, who was plowing. There were twelve yoke of oxen ahead of him, and he was with the twelfth. Elijah passed by him and threw his mantle over him" (1 Kings 19:19).

However strange it may have been, in that symbolic act Elisha heard the voice of God. He recognized God's call. When that mantle of Elijah was wrapped around him, in the warmth of that outer jacket, he felt the warm glow of the Spirit's presence. In the rustle of that mantle he heard the voice of God.

Why is it that some people seem to recognize the voice of God regularly in the everyday affairs of their lives, while others apparently don't hear that voice at all? John 12 contains an intriguing passage pertinent to this subject. Late in His ministry, Jesus was being rather introspective after being told that some Greeks wished to see Him, and He exclaimed, " 'Now my soul is troubled. And what should I say—"Father, save me from this hour"? No, it is for this reason that I have come to this hour' " (John 12:27).

Then Jesus prayed a very brief prayer, saying, " 'Father, glorify your name.' Then a voice came from heaven, 'I have glorified it, and I will glorify it again.' The crowd standing there heard it and said that it was thunder. Others said, 'An angel has spoken to him' " (John 12:28).

Why did some, when the divine voice responded to Jesus' prayer, hear only the rumbling noise of thunder, while others knew that heaven had spoken? Why do many people see their lives and achievements as simply a mixture of good luck, circumstance, and fortune, while others discern the guiding providence of God's hand? Why do thousands and thousands of individuals go through life and never recognize the call of God, while others speak to Him regularly and know that He answers? More important, what must we do to be sure that we recognize the voice of God, as did Elisha? There are several points relevant to this question drawn from the story of Elisha's call, points that we should remember in our attempt to hear the voice of God.

The first point is to remember that God's voice, His call to us, will not always come the way we might expect it. The Lord will not always speak to us in a manner we might anticipate. Elisha could certainly testify to this. Since God wanted him to do a special work, Elisha might have expected God to call him from a burning bush as He had Moses (see Exodus 3) or to communicate through a glorious, majestic vision as He would later do with Ezekiel (see Ezekiel 1). However, God's voice called Elisha through the simple act of placing a jacket around his shoulders.

Sometimes we want to dictate to God how He should speak to us, forgetting that God speaks in many different ways (Hebrews 1:1). I think of the experience of Elijah out on Mt. Horeb. He expected God to speak in the strong and mighty wind that tore at the mountain and blew the rocks around, "but the Lord was not in the wind" (1 Kings 19:11). Following the wind, Elijah held on for dear life as an earthquake shook the entire mountain. He anticipated a word from God, but to his surprise, "the Lord was not in the earthquake" (1 Kings 19:11). After the earthquake, an intense fire raced by, consuming everything flammable in its path, probably forcing Elijah to duck back in his cave, "but the Lord was not in the fire" (1 Kings 19:12). Following this, God spoke to him in a "still small voice" (1 Kings 19:12, KJV) or "a sound of sheer silence" (1 Kings 19:12).

Sometimes we are like Elijah. We expect God to speak to us through the spectacular and the miraculous. We expect a big extravaganza, forgetting that God speaks most often in that still, small voice.

A second point to remember is that God's voice will not always speak when we expect it. In fact, sometimes the voice of God calls when we least expect it. When Elisha went out to plow the field that day, he assumed it would be like any other day of plowing. He did not anticipate that it would be his last day as a farmer. When Peter, Andrew, James, and John cast their nets in the Sea of Galilee so long ago, they did not know that their careers as regular fishermen were about to come to an end, that Someone was about to summon them to be fishers for men (see Luke 5:1-11). When Matthew sat at his toll booth one day, he did not know that the Son of God Himself was about to issue that simple but profound call, "Follow Me" (see Luke 5:27, 28). The voice of God may speak at any time and in any place, and we must be ready to respond.

Sometimes people think that God speaks to His children only when they are nestled in a church pew, but evidence from Scripture reveals that God may speak at any time or in any place.

One day in 1856, in the small community of Waukon, Iowa, a discouraged former preacher name John Loughborough was perched on the top of a ladder. He was doing some carpentry work on a house. He did not expect that just at that moment, as he was on the ladder, the penetrating voice of God's messenger, Ellen G. White, would call to him saying, "What doest thou here, Elijah?" In other words, since God called you to preach, why are you doing the work of a carpenter?

Thankfully, John Loughborough responded to that voice that came to him unexpectedly. He rededicated himself to the gospel ministry, and for the next sixty-eight years he served as a preacher and evangelist, pioneering the Adventist work in both California and England.

A third point to remember is that it is important to listen closely. What if Elisha had been so preoccupied with his plowing that he didn't even notice what Elijah had done? What if he had just shrugged his shoulders and let that jacket fall to the ground? It was imperative for him to listen closely to recognize the voice of God calling.

During part of our courtship my wife and I had a cross-country relationship. One time during this long-distance phase, she answered the phone in her condominium and thought she heard my voice greeting her. Immediately, she went into what might be called the "lovey-dovey mode," saying with a syrupy voice, "I've missed you so much. I'm so glad you called." Unfortunately for her, it was my brother—who sounds a great deal like me—on the other end of the line. Having a sense of humor, he let the conversation go on a little while, to my future wife's embarrassment. She needed to listen closely in order to make out whose voice it really was.

Even so, God does not always declare, "This is God" when He wishes to speak to us. Sometimes He just speaks, and unless we are listening carefully, we might mistake the voice of God for another voice.

Related to the previous point is the fact that listening closely to God includes tuning out other voices, eliminating the plethora of voices that compete with God for our attention. I am an amateur radio operator. Sometimes I have talked to people halfway around the world and their voice comes in clear as a bell. At other times, though, I can't understand what the person is saying, because another voice is "walking" on theirs. In other words, there is too much interference, too many voices.

We need to listen closely for God's voice, tuning out the interference. If there is one Bible text that we especially need as a watchword in our hurry, scurry, and worry, hustle-bustle society of the twenty-first century and the new millennium, it is the one found in the forty-sixth psalm: " 'Be still, and know that I am God!' " (Psalm 46:10). We might paraphrase this to say that if we will be still and listen, we will know Him as our God and have a personal relationship with Him. We would do well to make this verse our motto, placing it on the doorposts of our home (see Deuteronomy 6:9).

Let us now consider the second characteristic of Elisha that is worthy of imitation: Not only did he listen to the voice of God, but also he responded to that call. There are those who hear God's voice, and even know it to be a voice from heaven, but who never respond. This was certainly not the case with Elisha.

The Bible describes his response this way: "He left the oxen, ran after Elijah, and said, 'Let me kiss my father and my mother, and then I will follow you.' Then Elijah said to him, 'Go back again; for what have I done to you?' He returned from following him, took the yoke of oxen, and slaughtered them; using the equipment from the oxen, he boiled their flesh, and gave it to the people, and they ate. Then he set out and followed Elijah, and became his servant" (1 Kings 19:20, 21).

As Elisha prepared to respond to his call, Elijah tested him. We might paraphrase him as saying, "Settle down. What's all the excitement?" But undeterred by this test, Elisha responded with commitment.

Let us examine several aspects of this commitment. It is safe to say that Elisha responded with complete commitment.

Perhaps you have heard the saying, "Don't burn all your bridges behind you." This metaphor arose from military strategy. To elaborate, an army that is advancing had better not burn all the bridges that it uses to travel across rivers because the time might just come when the army needs to retreat. It only makes sense.

This saying is excellent advice in some areas of life. For example, if you get a new job that you think will make you happier than your old position, there is no need to go to your previous boss on your last day at work and say, "I've had it up to here with this job. I'm finished!" Even though you might feel that way at times, you would be better not to burn that bridge. What if you should need a letter of recommendation at some future point? What if you should need to get your old job back again? You'd better not burn that bridge!

But when it comes to making a commitment to the Lord, Elisha burned his bridges and so should we. The Bible tells us he started a fire with his farming tools, and killed his oxen. That may seem to you like going overboard, but Elisha was making an emphatic statement: "I won't be needing these anymore." There was to be no turning back.

When Jesus was asked what is the greatest commandment in the law, he replied, " ' "You shall love the Lord your God with all your heart, and with all your soul, and with all your mind, and with all your strength" ' " (Mark 12:30). One of the most notable things about this commandment is the fourfold use of the word "all." We are called upon to love God completely, with all our heart, all our soul, all our mind, and all our strength. Jesus' emphasis was on complete commitment.

Perhaps the greatest problem facing the Christian church today is that of incomplete commitment. Those who profess to be Christians are not totally committed to Jesus Christ. Have you considered the great revival that could take place if all whose names were on the church membership roll made a complete commitment to Jesus Christ? Sad to say, we are prone to keep one hand on the world, while reaching out to

Jesus with the other. We don't burn our bridges, just in case we want to go back over them. Whatever bridges are still standing in our lives, we must burn them down and make a complete commitment.

Not only did Elisha respond with a complete commitment, he also responded with a public commitment. As Scripture indicates, he boiled the flesh of his oxen and he served it to everyone there. We might say he was the host of a "fellowship dinner." He wanted to state publicly that he was responding to the call of God.

In this day and age we tend to diminish the importance of a public commitment. We tend to use pious-sounding phrases like "Religion is a personal matter" and "God knows the heart." There is truth in these statements, but it is also true that the Lord proclaimed, " 'Everyone therefore who acknowledges me before others, I also will acknowledge before my Father in heaven; but whoever denies me before others, I also will deny before my Father in heaven' " (Matthew 10:32).

I can remember the evening many years ago when a certain minister made an appeal for those who wanted to give their hearts to the Lord to step forward. I heard the voice of God speaking to my heart, asking for a public response. However, I was sitting near the back and there were many other people there, including some schoolmates. What would they think? Had it been only the minister and me, it would have been much easier to step out into the aisle. Though it wasn't easy to get out of my seat, I'm glad the Spirit continued to speak to me and gave me strength to step out for Jesus. It made an impact on me to make a public response.

Someone might ask, "Why is it important to respond with a public commitment?" There are two basic reasons. First, it highlights the significance of the decision to follow the Lord. It gives that decision the importance that it deserves. When at a wedding, the bride and groom stand before God, the minister, and all their relatives and friends, and pledge a lifelong love to one another, it underscores the importance of the occasion.

Second, a public response serves as an example to others. It encourages them to step forward in faith and make a public response also.

In a sense, we are not really disciples until we have made a public commitment. I think of Nicodemus, who came to Jesus by night, wanting to learn more about this new teacher (see John 3). It was good that he came, but to tell the truth, he was only a seeker and not really a disciple until the Friday afternoon he came openly and gently took the bruised and battered body of Jesus down from the cross (see John 19:38-40).

Today, God's voice speaks, as certainly as He spoke to Elisha in yonder days. I cannot tell you what the voice is saying. Only you know. Maybe He is inviting you to have a closer walk with Him. Perhaps your devotional life has slipped and you haven't been taking time to listen to the Lord. He is inviting you to spend time with Him on a daily basis. Maybe you and your spouse live under the same roof, but to put it bluntly, you don't love one another the way you once did, and the Lord is challenging you to heal that wounded relationship.

I don't know what the still, small voice is saying, but I do know it is speaking today. Speaking to you. Are you listening? Are you willing to commit? What is your answer today?

CHAPTER

When Crisis Comes

2 Kings 18; 19

It was late May 1940, during the early months of World War II. A moment of crisis had arrived for the Allied armies. The Nazi juggernaut had already swept across Poland in the east and devastated the Netherlands in the west. Then the German army had raced around the main mass of the French forces by going through Belgium. The left flank of the French army crumbled in the face of the German advance, leaving nearly a half million British, French, and Dutch soldiers trapped on the coast of northern France near the city of Dunkirk.

The situation looked hopeless for the Allied soldiers. They were outmaneuvered and outgunned. The German army was closing in rapidly, and the sea blocked their retreat. There appeared to be no way out. It seemed that this huge mass of Allied soldiers would soon be either dead or prisoners of the Nazis.

However, the Nazis had not counted on the determination and will of the British people. In "Operation Dynamo," one of the greatest military evacuations of all time, some 860 British vessels, including yachts, fishing boats, barges, and basically any other kind of seaworthy craft, began going back and forth across the English Channel to rescue as many soldiers as possible. Though enduring withering attack from German aircraft, they were able to rescue some 360,000 Allied soldiers, providing an important moral victory at a critical moment in the war. The term "Dunkirk" became a metaphor for "crisis" and a reminder of how one might successfully respond in time of crisis.

Some twenty-seven centuries ago, a "Dunkirk," a moment of crisis, arrived for King Hezekiah of Judah. It was also occasioned by an invasion of a foreign power, the menacing army of Assyria. In order to understand Hezekiah's crisis, a little background information is helpful. Prior to Hezekiah's reign, his father Ahaz, in an ill-advised move, had invited Tiglath-pileser III, king of Assyria, to protect him from the armies of Aram and Israel. Tiglath had complied, but the assistance had come at a heavy cost. It was like inviting the fox to guard the hen house. Not only were the people of Judah assessed heavy tribute, they were also expected to embrace Assyrian worship forms (see 2 Kings 16). It was a bargain with the devil, and it took a dreadful toll on the spiritual welfare of the people.

But Hezekiah was no Ahaz. Desiring to assert political independence and to escape from the clutches of foreign domination, recognizing the peril of worshiping foreign gods and the need of complete commitment to Yahweh the true God, "Hezekiah rebelled against the king of Assyria and would not serve him" (2 Kings 18:7).

It was a risky move. Assyria was the most powerful nation of its day, boasting a powerful military force and possessing a hunger for foreign conquest. It was the nation that had annihilated Judah's sister kingdom Israel, destroying the capital city of Samaria and sending the people into exile around 722 B.C. And it did not take Hezekiah's challenge lightly. Sennacherib, the king, attacked Judah, defeated most of the fortified cites (2 Kings 18:13), and sent Hezekiah an ultimatum that basically said, "Jerusalem is history. Your reign is over. Surrender or else."

It was one of the gravest crises in the history of the people of Jerusalem. Assyria was in no mood to parley. Things looked bleak. From a human perspective, there was no hope. The comparatively tiny kingdom of Judah seemed helpless before the Assyrian juggernaut. But when all was said and done, when the crisis was over, when the smoke had cleared, the Lord had defended His people, the Assyrian army lay in ruins, and their nemesis Sennacherib lay slain in the temple of his god (see 2 Kings 19:32-37).

A key question to consider in exploring this biblical story is the following: What can we learn from this story about how to deal with a crisis? What should we do when a crisis comes? This is not a moot issue. For at some time or another, each of God's children faces a crisis. It may be a health crisis in the family. Perhaps a parent or a spouse is diagnosed with a serious, possibly fatal, disease. It may be an economic crisis. Maybe we have worked at the same office or factory for many years and the bottom falls out on our economic well being when we receive an unexpected pink slip at work. It may be a crisis in our marriage relationship. We never planned for things to turn out this way, but one day we hear our marriage partner say that they need some time alone. Or it may be a spiritual crisis. Perhaps our walk with the Lord seems to have stagnated, or we just don't see God's presence with all the events happening in our lives.

What should we do in a moment of crisis? The story of Hezekiah's crisis and how he dealt with it provides some helpful guidance and suggestions to us as we deal with crises in our lives.

First, it is important that those who are in a crisis not be captive to the past. This was certainly true of Hezekiah. Though his father Ahaz was an enthusiastic supporter of Assyria and imported Assyrian worship forms (see 2 Kings 16:10-18), Hezekiah was not beholden to this pattern. It was important for him, even during the early days of his reign, to set out on a new pathway and declare his allegiance to the God of heaven (see 2 Kings 18:1-6).

I have known a number of church members who seem to spend a lot of time imprisoned by their past. Perhaps they claim their upbringing was too legalistic or maybe they claim the church was too unloving. Or perhaps they were "invited" to leave a Christian school and they are still decrying the injustice of it all. But for whatever reason, they spend a lot of time and energy flailing away at the past and never really able to enjoy a relationship with God or fellowship with His church. They have an interest in spiritual things but they are only partially committed. They live their lives on the fringes, not really in the church but not really in the world.

I am always encouraged in this regard when I think of my maternal grandfather whom I affectionately called "Poppy." If anyone had a reason for bitterness, he did. His beloved mother had died when he was six, and for the rest of his growing-up years he had a stepmother who inflicted horrors unimaginable. However, his settled conviction was that life was too short to harbor any bitterness and that the twofold privilege of a personal relationship with his Lord and belonging to the Adventist Church more than surpassed any challenges life may have brought his way.

This lesson from the life of Hezekiah and from the experience of my grandfather is important today: Let's not be stuck in the rut of our past. As the Lord declared through the prophet, "Do not remember the former things, or consider the things of old. I am about to do a new thing" (Isaiah 43:18, 19).

A second point worth noting from how Hezekiah dealt with a crisis is that preparation for a crisis begins before the crisis. When the Assyrian army invaded his comparatively tiny kingdom, Hezekiah would have been in a bad way had he exhibited no spiritual commitment prior to this crisis. He would have had no reservoir of faith on which to draw, nowhere to turn. However, as noted above, his reign had already been distinguished by his faithfulness to God. The Bible states, "He trusted in the Lord the God of Israel; so that there was no one like him among all the kings of Judah after him, or among those who were before him. For he held fast to the Lord; he did not depart from following him but kept the commandments that the Lord commanded Moses" (2 Kings 18:5, 6).

Sometimes Christians place a great emphasis on the testing times that occur for all Christians at some time or another. They may even say something like this: "Character is formed in times of crisis." However, this is not really true. It is more correct to say that character is formed in the regular daily events of life, but it is *revealed* in times of crisis. There is a difference in the two perspectives.

Some Christians have spent a lot of time wondering how they might respond in the great Time of Trouble immediately before the Lord returns. They inquire of themselves, *Will I be faithful?* The best answer to that question is seen in how that individual responds to the tests and challenges that occur on a regular basis. Do they turn to God? Depend on Him? Trust in His love and care?

As a college teacher, I have some students who wait until just before the final exam to spend any time studying. There are other students who keep up with their assignments faithfully throughout the class. As you might surmise, the latter group tends to do better.

It is true in the Christian life also. Preparation for a crisis begins prior to the crisis. It is ongoing, taking place on a regular basis. We are preparing every day for any crisis we might face in the future.

A third point we can learn from the response of Hezekiah to the crisis posed by the Assyrian invasion is that a crisis presents an opportunity to draw closer to God. Though as indicated above, Hezekiah was already a devout follower of the Lord, the peril he faced called him to an even deeper commitment. When the Assyrian army threatened his nation with extinction, Hezekiah sought God more fully, more fervently, in a way he had not sought Him before (see 2 Kings 19).

Now we certainly shouldn't wait until a time of crisis arrives before forming a relationship with the Lord. However, since we never reach a plateau in our relationship with God (see Phil. 3:12-14), since God is always inviting us to have a deeper relationship with Him, when crises do occur we should view them as an invitation to draw even closer to God.

We might even say that there is a spiritual dimension to every crisis in life. In Hezekiah's day, the crisis may have appeared to be a secular one, for Sennacherib was ostensibly challenging the people of Judah. However, Hezekiah saw the attack for what it really was, a challenge to their God. He prayed, " 'Incline your ear, O Lord, and hear; open your eyes, O Lord, and see; hear the words of Sennacherib, which he has sent to mock the living God' " (2 Kings 19:16). This is true also of the crises that we face. Whatever area of our lives might be the specific focus of the crisis, whether relationships or health or finances, it also has a spiritual dimension, and we ignore that dimension at our peril.

This was certainly the perspective of the prophet Joel. Though the specific crisis that served as the occasion for his prophecy was an unprecedented, devastating locust plague that threatened the very existence of the nation (see Joel 1:2-12), he viewed this disaster as a summons to get right with God. The prophet declared: "Yet even now, says the Lord, return to me with all your heart, with fasting, with weeping, and with mourning; rend your hearts and not your clothing. Return to the Lord your God" (Joel 2:12, 13).

It might be worthwhile to observe the specific steps Hezekiah took in drawing closer to God. He humbled himself in an attitude of repentance (see 2 Kings 19:1), and he consulted God's messenger Isaiah for any word from the Lord (2 Kings 19:2). Additionally, he "went up to the house of the Lord and spread it [the menacing message he had received from Sennacherib] before the Lord" (2 Kings 19:14). Finally, he prayed a deeply meaningful prayer, taking the crisis to the throne room of the universe (2 Kings 19:15-19). None of these steps is antiquated or irrelevant today. They serve as a good paradigm of how we might draw closer to God while in our own crisis.

A fourth point we can learn, related to the previous, is that in every crisis a key issue is trust. A quality that distinguished Hezekiah, an integral component in the deliverance of his nation, was his trust in God. Ironically, after telling us that Hezekiah "trusted in the Lord" (2 Kings 18:5), the biblical writer quotes Sennacherib's messengers repeatedly inquiring as to the object of Hezekiah's trust and challenging whether it would make any difference that he does trust in the Lord. For instance, one of the Assyrian commanders asked Hezekiah, " 'On whom do you now rely [Heb., 'trust']?' " (2 Kings 18:20). Additionally, the same official shouted to the people of Jerusalem, " ' "Do not let Hezekiah make you rely [Heb., "trust"] on the Lord" ' " (2 Kings 18:30).

As one scholar notes, the noun or verb "trust" (Heb., *batakh*) appears ten times in the biblical description of this crisis (2 Kings 18; 19) and only three times in the rest of Genesis through 2 Kings (Hamilton, *Handbook on the Historical Books,* 458). The frequent appearance of this word, particularly in key places in this narrative, is meant to underscore that the key issue in this story is trust. Whom did Hezekiah trust in this moment of crisis? Sennacherib accused him of trusting in Egypt to deliver him (2 Kings 18:21), but such was not the case. The careful reader already knows from the outset of the story that Hezekiah's trust was where it had been for many years of his life: in Yahweh, the only true God (2 Kings 18:5). This is what makes the difference in the outcome of the story.

And what of us today? When crises arise, in whom do we trust? In whom is our confidence? When the night seems dark around us, when we don't understand what is happening in our lives, when God and His ways don't make sense to us, are we still willing to rely on God, to trust in Him? Though cold, lonely, abandoned by some of his friends, and expecting to die the death of a martyr (see 2 Timothy 4), the apostle Paul was still able to declare, "I know the one in whom I have put my trust, and I am sure that he is able to guard until that day what I have entrusted to him" (2 Timothy 1:12).

A fifth point to learn from the crisis faced by Hezekiah is not to be alarmed by outward appearances. In Hezekiah's case, this was easier said than done. From a human point of view, there was every reason to be alarmed when the Assyrian king threatened the city of Jerusalem and its inhabitants. The Assyrian army had already decimated a number of other nations (see 2 Kings 18:12, 13), including Judah's sister nation of Israel (see 2 Kings 18:9-12). It was the most powerful military force in the Near Eastern world. It was known for its rapaciousness and cruelty. It seemed that no one could stand in its way, let alone the little kingdom of Judah. But this is reasoning from a human point of view.

Similarly, in the contest between David and Goliath, David faced overwhelming odds. Goliath would have been a million-to-one favorite, a shoo-in. But to take this perspective would be to forget the truth expressed in David's stirring speech: " 'You come to me with sword and spear and javelin; but I come to you in the name of the Lord of hosts, the God of the armies of Israel, whom you have defied. This very day the Lord will deliver you into my hand . . . that all this assembly may know that the Lord does not save by sword and spear; for the battle is the Lord's and he will give you into our hand' " (1 Samuel 17:45-47). In this speech, David spoke of what he needed most of all—not smooth stones, not an accurate aim, but, stated simply, an unflinching confidence that God would grant him victory over Goliath.

Often we face crises that on the surface seem formidable or even insurmountable. From a human perspective, there appears to be no hope of a satisfactory resolution. The crisis hangs over us like the sword of Damocles, threatening to undo us. In times like these, we need to remember not to be concerned about outward appearances. We need to recall that again and again in the Bible, God has brought hope to a hopeless situation and snatched victory out of the mouth of defeat.

Because we are intimidated by the situation, sometimes we rely on all the wrong things in times of crisis. We trust in our own intelligence, our own strength, our own financial resources, or the like, thinking this will resolve the crisis. But if truth be told, God doesn't have to have any of those in order to bring resolution. What He does need is for us to open our hearts to Him, to place our confidence in Him, and to trust in His ability to resolve the crisis in His own time and His own way.

In Hezekiah's case, he didn't need more soldiers or stronger city walls. What he did need was what he had—a relationship with a God who had heard the taunts and mockings of Sennacherib and was about ready to act on behalf of His people (see 2 Kings 19:20-28).

The final point to learn from Hezekiah's crisis is one of the grandest truths of Scripture, namely, that God is the Savior of His people. It is true that He allowed them to be threatened in the days of Hezekiah. Their peril was grave. The threat was genuine. It drove Hezekiah to take his problem to the Lord (2 Kings 19:14). It drove him to his knees in prayer (2 Kings 19:15). God was his last, best hope.

But what a last, best hope to have. At Judah's moment of extremity, God had a word for them regarding His plans: " 'Therefore thus says the Lord concerning the king of Assyria: He shall not come into this city, shoot an arrow there, come before it with a shield, or cast up a siege ramp against it. By the way that he came, by the same shall he return; he shall not come into this city, says the Lord. For I will defend this city to save it, for my own sake and for the sake of my servant David' " (2 Kings 19:32-34).

The next thing we know, the vaunted Assyrian war machine lay in ruins and the arrogant Assyrian king lay dead in his temple, worshiping a god that could provide no protection even while in that god's house (see 2 Kings 19:35-37). Of interest is the vivid contrast this latter scene presents with Hezekiah's visit to the temple of the Lord, which led to the Lord saving His people (see 2 Kings 19:14-19).

What God did so long ago in the crisis in Hezekiah's time is a fore-taste of what He will do at the final crisis in earth's history. Though the people of God will face great peril and be threatened with death (see Revelation 13), though it will seem that overwhelming odds are against them, the Lord will step in at the moment of greatest extremity and save His people who keep the commandments of God and have the faith of Jesus (see Revelation 14:12).

Yes, ultimately, the Lord is the Savior of His people, their Redeemer *par excellence.* This is the great truth highlighted by the story of Hezekiah, the great truth highlighted by the totality of Scripture. When crises arise, as they most certainly will, the knowledge that we have a Savior sustains us and gives us strength to face any challenge that might come our way.

This chapter has talked a good bit about Hezekiah and his response to the Assyrian crisis, but to tell the truth, that's not the main point. The important issue today is not how Hezekiah handled his crisis but how we will handle ours. When a crisis comes, what will we do? Where will we turn? And most importantly, in whom do we trust?

CHAPTER 10

Home in His Vineyard

1 Kings 21

It took a bit of searching in the city of Rome, but I finally found it. It was off the beaten path, not frequented by tourists, as were the majestic sites of St. Peter's Basilica and the Sistine Chapel, but I felt a real need to see it. Below the church of San Giuseppe dei Falegnami (St. Joseph of the Carpenters) is a dungeon known as the Mamertine Prison. According to tradition, both Peter and Paul were held here before being martyred for their faith around A.D. 66.

Upon finding it and going down into the dungeon, I was pleased to have a few undisturbed minutes for reflection and prayer while I was there. I pondered what it must have been like for the great apostles to spend their last earthly days in that cell. How did they feel? What were their sentiments before going to their deaths?

One conclusion I came to as I stood there in the Mamertine is that God's faithful children will only receive their final vindication from God. They must be willing to wait for that time. They must have faith that God will have the final word, and His word is the one that really counts! Human rulers may impugn their characters, challenge their integrity, mistreat and abuse them, but God will have the final say-so, and ultimately He will vindicate His children.

Often, they are not vindicated at the time. Far from it! You see, martyrdom is not necessarily glorious for the person experiencing it. Not at the time they are going to their death anyway. While later generations laud the martyrs, write books about them (see the earlier *Foxe's Book of Martyrs* and the more recent *Jesus Freaks*), and celebrate their complete commitment to God, the pathway to martyrdom is often lonely for the one walking it.

The Mamertine Prison is exhibit A of this. A later legend said that Peter caused a spring to bubble up into the cell and used the water to baptize his two prison guards, but this is probably just an example of someone inventing a story in an attempt to embellish the memory of the great apostle and make his final days in prison sound rather glorious. If truth were told, the Mamertine is a dank, dark underground dungeon that, from a human perspective, would have been a lonely and miserable place to live out one's last days. We catch some of the loneliness of Paul when we read the final chapter of his last will and testament (see 2 Timothy 4).

The point I am making is this. Should you be called to yield up your life out of faithfulness to principle or commitment to God, don't expect huge crowds to be cheering you on. If anything, they will probably be cheering on the executioner. Don't expect your noble achievement to be recognized as such at the time. Rather, you must be willing to wait for God's vindication. You must be willing to trust that He will speak the final word, and it is His word that really counts. Whatever your earthly circumstances might be, however you might be treated, whatever others should say about you and do to you, God's perspective on your situation is the one that counts, and in the final analysis, God will vindicate His children. The Lord has promised, " 'Be faithful until death, and I will give you the crown of life' " (Revelation 2:10).

This hope of final vindication is what made it bearable for Stephen as he felt the rocks pelting his body, for John the Baptist as he was led out of his dungeon to the chopping block. Though there were things they didn't understand, things they probably had questions about (Why doesn't God deliver me? Why is He allowing this to happen?), they were willing to rest their case in God and await His vindication. To do otherwise would have been to sacrifice principle, to manifest less than complete commitment to God.

Another man who awaits God's final vindication is Naboth of Jezreel. One of the saddest stories in the Old Testament is the story of Naboth and how his vineyard was taken from him unjustly. It is a story in which the unfairness and injustice leap out at the reader. It is a story in which the unfortunate victim must rely on God for his future vindication. The story goes like this.

Naboth, a man of Jezreel, owned a vineyard that was situated next to Ahab's palace in Jezreel (see 1 Kings 21:1). Evidently, Ahab had two palaces, one in Samaria (see 1 Kings 20:43) and a second winter palace in the warmer Jezreel valley for when it was chilly in Samaria. However much he possessed, though, he was not satisfied with it, for he desired to add Naboth's vineyards to his holdings. He probably thought it would enhance the beauty and value of his winter palace and would make a nice buffer zone between land held by commoners and the king's palace. But for whatever reason, he decided he wanted to acquire it. Notice how his offer to Naboth starts out in the biblical record, "And Ahab said to Naboth, 'Give me your vineyard' " (1 Kings 21:2).

The first two words of Ahab's statement, "Give me," suggest from the very outset that Ahab had an "I" problem. Just as is the case with the description of Lucifer in Isaiah 14:12-14. In just three short verses, Lucifer uses some form of the first person pronoun ("I," "my," or "myself") seven times. "I will do this," "I myself will do that," he says. It has been noted that he had an "I" problem—he couldn't see past himself. These same two words, "Give me," are the first two words of the prodigal son's demand of his father as he prepares to leave home (see Luke 15:12). The antidote to this focus on self is to learn the secret the apostle Paul learned so long ago, namely to be content in whatever circumstances one finds oneself (see Philippians 4:12).

Now it is true that Ahab made an eminently reasonable offer for Naboth's property. He told Naboth, " 'I will give you a better vineyard for it; or, if it seems good to you, I will give you its value in money' " (1 Kings 21:2). But however reasonable the offer, Naboth wasn't interested. He didn't want to sell. And his lack of interest wasn't a ploy to negotiate for a higher price. There was to be no deal for this land. "Naboth said to Ahab, 'The Lord forbid that I should give you my ancestral inheritance' " (1 Kings 21:3).

Naboth felt that it was not in harmony with God's will for him to sell the land that had belonged in his family for some time. Perhaps he had an emotional attachment to this property. Additionally, he may have in mind divine injunctions such as Leviticus 25:23-25, which indicates that land is not to pass permanently out of the possession of its owner. But for whatever the exact reason, Naboth rejected Ahab's offer.

Predictably, Ahab was not happy to be denied this property. Imitating his pattern from the previous chapter when he had heard something he didn't like (see 1 Kings 20:42, 43), he went home and pouted like a sulking child. "Ahab went home resentful and sullen because of what Naboth the Jezreelite had said to him; for he had said, 'I will not give you my ancestral inheritance.' He lay down on his bed, turned away his face, and would not eat" (1 Kings 21:4).

Soon Jezebel came upon the scene. Finding Ahab sulking on his bed, she asked him what the problem was. It is interesting that Ahab in his reply did not quote Naboth accurately. He mentioned nothing about Naboth stating that the Lord wouldn't want him to make the sale. He simply quoted him as saying, " ' "I will not give you my vineyard" ' " (1 Kings 21:6).

Not that it would have mattered to Jezebel anyway. True to form, Jezebel was a person of action. As was the case after the display of God's power on Mt. Carmel, she was completely undaunted by forbidding circumstances (see 1 Kings 19:1, 2). She did not view Naboth's refusal to sell as an insurmountable obstacle to adding his vineyard to the royal holdings. Not at all. In her view, she and Ahab ruled Israel and could do what they wanted. "His wife Jezebel said to him, 'Do you now govern Israel? Get up, eat some food, and be cheerful; I will give you the vineyard of Naboth the Jezreelite' " (1 Kings 21:7).

Of course, from the biblical perspective, there is a deep flaw in this philosophy. Ultimately, as Gideon declared so long ago, the Lord was to be the King over His people (see Judges 8:23). His principles of justice and fairness were to prevail. His laws were to be upheld. The strong were not to oppress the weak, and they were not to subvert the justice system, as the biblical prophets make abundantly clear. Yet that is just what happened in this situation.

Evidently, Jezebel followed the philosophy of "might makes right." Her guiding principle was that if Ahab wanted the vineyard of Naboth, then he should have it. After all, he was king and the king should get what he wants without hindrance or impediment. If Naboth wouldn't sell his vineyard, then Jezebel would get it some other way.

So she came up with a strategy to attain by foul means what was otherwise unavailable to her. Two false witnesses were to be seated near Naboth at a public occasion. They would accuse him of cursing God and the king, both of which were considered capital offenses at this time. Then Naboth would be taken out and receive his "just sentence." It all seemed very simple.

And all went according to plan. "The two scoundrels came in and sat opposite him; and the scoundrels brought a charge against Naboth, in the presence of the people, saying, 'Naboth cursed God and the king.' So they took him outside the city, and stoned him to death" (1 Kings 21:13).

When Jezebel received the news, she didn't bat an eye. She went and told Ahab that Naboth was now dead and his vineyard was there for Ahab's taking. She even showed regard for her husband's sensitivities and spared him the details of Naboth's undoing so he would not have to know how Naboth came to his end and of his own connection with it (see 1 Kings 21:15). What a thoughtful, caring woman!

Several points should be made at this juncture in the story. First, the cruelty and injustice of it all leap out at the reader. What a profoundly unfair act! I wonder what poor Naboth thought while being dragged away to his death, while being pelted with stones. Did he have some inkling that this was all happening because he refused to sell his vineyard to the king? Had he had some premonition since that refusal that his decision could come back to make things difficult for him?

I remember my own feelings several years back upon learning of a patently unfair verdict in a murder case. The accused was obviously guilty.

It seemed so obvious. The evidence was overwhelming. Fact after fact pointed in the direction of the accused. Yet in a miscarriage of justice, he was declared not guilty. It was profoundly disturbing, an indictment of the whole justice system. I felt sick inside to hear the results.

And this is how one feels about the murder of Naboth. This case screams out for redress, it calls out for Naboth's vindication. Truly it could be said about Naboth, as had been said about Abel so long ago, that his blood cried out to God from the ground (see Genesis 4:10).

Another point worth noting is the complicity of the city leaders in Jezebel's wicked plot. Twice the biblical text makes the point that the elders and the misnamed "nobles" cooperated with her plan. The letter detailing the plan was addressed to them (see 1 Kings 21:8), and the Bible tells us that the elders and the nobles of Jezreel "did as Jezebel had sent word to them" (1 Kings 21:11).

This fact underscores for us that monstrous acts of evil are rarely done by a single person. The atrocities of Nazi Germany were not wrought by Adolf Hitler alone. All who assist or cooperate, or who even stand by silently without raising a voice of protest while evil is transpiring, as did Saul of Tarsus while Stephen was being stoned, are held responsible for what they refuse to oppose. The elders and nobles of Jezreel bore some responsibility for what happened to poor Naboth. They had complicity. This raises the question of whether there is some evil or injustice to which we have some connection, some moral wrong that we should oppose instead of being compliant or complicit.

An additional point from this story is how wrongdoing spirals out of control. Sin leads to more sin. What was said of chips in the old commercial is also true of disobedience: You can't stop with just one. One wrong act leads to another. The commandments of God are interconnected in a remarkable way.

One author points out how Ahab and Jezebel broke at least five of the Ten Commandments: They dishonored Naboth's parents by unlawfully taking what they had passed along to their son as the family inheritance (commandment five); they murdered (commandment six); they stole

95

(commandment seven); they arranged to bear false witness, literally against a neighbor (commandment nine); and Ahab coveted (commandment ten) (Victor Hamilton, *Handbook on the Historical Books,* 440).

This should sound a note of warning to us. Sometimes we minimize the impact of a wrong action we are about to take. One little lie on my tax return won't hurt, we say. One brief glance at a pornographic image on the Web won't do any lasting damage. Though this video is not appropriate for a Christian, one bad video won't cause harm. It behooves us to remember that disobedience always leads to more disobedience, sin always leads to more sin. It was thus for Ahab and Jezebel, and so it is for us.

We now move to Ahab and his actions in the aftermath of Naboth's murder. When Jezebel told him, " 'Naboth is not alive, but dead' " (1 Kings 21:15), he showed no curiosity about how Naboth died. He asked no questions. If Jezebel followed the philosophy of "might makes right," perhaps his guiding principle was "what you don't know can't hurt you." Presumably, Naboth had been in good health when Ahab had tendered his offer to buy, but Ahab expressed no surprise upon learning of his demise. Perhaps Ahab was suspicious, but it was better from his perspective not to confirm his suspicions.

So off he went to take a look at "his" new property. "As soon as Ahab heard that Naboth was dead, Ahab set out to go down to the vineyard of Naboth the Jezreelite, to take possession of it" (1 Kings 21:16). But if he thought he was going to be able to enjoy this ill-gotten property in peace, to be able to enjoy the view without disturbance, he was in for a big surprise.

As is always the case, God was aware of what had taken place. He was still on the throne. He had seen the perplexed look on Naboth's face as he had been dragged away to his death. He had heard this faithful man's dying cries. Though He had chosen not to intervene and spare faithful Naboth's earthly life, He was about to intrude into the situation. What was said of David's sin with Bathsheba could also be said of Ahab and Jezebel's actions in this case: But the thing that they had done "displeased the Lord" (2 Samuel 11:27).

The Lord spoke to Elijah and gave him an incisive message to deliver to Ahab. Elijah would find him in "the vineyard of Naboth," the Lord said. This is a telling comment. Even though Naboth was dead, according to the divine perspective, the vineyard belonged to him. Also, Elijah was to accuse Ahab of murdering Naboth in order to take his vineyard. Though Ahab might have thought his hands were clean and that he could deny direct involvement in the plot, he was no more blameless than was Pontius Pilate. And finally, Elijah was to declare the tragic fate that awaited Ahab in the future.

As Ahab went on his initial stroll through what he now claimed as his vineyard, the sight of another man must have startled him. It was an old acquaintance who had come to pay a visit. Ahab's greeting, if it can be called such, indicates his awareness that the encounter will not be a pleasant one. "Ahab said to Elijah, 'Have you found me, O my enemy?'" (1 Kings 21:20).

In reply, Elijah minced no words. He pronounced judgment upon the entire family of Ahab. Because of his wickedness, his dynasty would come to a disastrous and cataclysmic conclusion. There would be no honor in death for anyone from this family, Jezebel in particular (see 1 Kings 21:21-24). Though in response to Ahab's humbling himself (see 1 Kings 21:27-29), judgment might wait and even seem to linger, it would not be denied.

What else could be expected but judgment when the overall assessment of Ahab's reign is as follows: "Indeed, there was no one like Ahab, who sold himself to do what was evil in the sight of the LORD, urged on by his wife Jezebel. He acted most abominably in going after idols, as the Amorites had done, whom the LORD drove out before the Israelites" (1 Kings 21:25, 26).

And indeed, the story of Ahab and his supporting cast played out to its expected denouement. Ahab came to an inglorious end (see 1 Kings 22:37-38), as did Jezebel (see 2 Kings 9:35) and the rest of Ahab's descendants (see 2 Kings 10). And from our perspective, knowing the injustice that had been wreaked upon innocent Naboth, we might say they got what they deserved. God gave them their just deserts.

But there is one problem that needs to be cleared up. While Ahab and Jezebel may have reaped what they had sown, poor Naboth wasn't around to see it. His last memory was of being falsely accused of cursing God and the king and being pelted with rocks. What can we say about that?

There are a couple of things to remember. One, God hasn't forgotten Naboth. He cared about this faithful Israelite. While most people then didn't know him, while the city leaders obviously considered him expendable, while even most contemporary Christians have forgotten his name, such is not the case with God. As the psalmist declared, "Precious in the sight of the Lord is the death of his faithful ones" (Psalm 116:15). Since this is true, God must have carefully noted the tragic end of faithful Naboth.

Second, I like to imagine a scene from the future when Isaiah's depiction of the glorious new creation will be realized. Speaking of the redeemed, the prophet stated, "They shall build houses and inhabit them; they shall plant vineyards and eat their fruit. They shall not build and another inhabit; they shall not plant and another eat" (Isaiah 65:21, 22).

I believe that this prophecy has a special application for faithful Naboth. I can picture the Lord Himself leading Naboth to a vineyard He has prepared especially for him. It is much more beautiful and gorgeous than the one Naboth had next to Ahab's palace. It is his forevermore, granted him by God Himself. God might say, "Naboth, remember that vineyard you had back on earth? I loaned it to you temporarily. But what you see now, this is your vineyard. It is yours today, yours tomorrow, yours forever."

And with that, God will give ultimate vindication to Naboth and all His faithful children. Whatever happened on earth is past. Ahab and Jezebel, along with all their spiritual descendants, those who were willing to step on others and take advantage of them to achieve their own selfish goals, will be no more. God has judged them, and He will speak the final word on behalf of His people.

And what is that final word? "Welcome home, all of My children. Cruelty, torture, and martyrdom are past. The perpetrators of such wickedness are no more. Your vindication has arrived. I claim you as Mine, My own treasure. Forever you will enjoy My presence. You are home now, home in your own vineyard. Welcome home."

CHAPTER 11

When You Come to the End of Life's Journey

2 Kings 13

The aging prophet groaned inwardly. His old bones creaked as he swung his legs to the side of the bed and placed his feet on the cold, hard floor. He waited there for a few moments, sitting on the edge of the bed, trying to muster enough strength to face a new day. It was not as easy to get up as it had once been. Bones and muscles aged eighty years did not function as well as they had when he was in his twenties.

As he sat there on the edge of the bed, Elisha began to reminisce, his mind traveling back through the many years of service he had rendered to God. He could still clearly remember that day more than fifty years before when Elijah had come upon him while he was plowing in the field and had slipped the mantle of service over his shoulders. Elisha had responded with complete commitment to this symbolic act in which he had heard the call of God (see 1 Kings 19:19-21). He recalled Elijah's ascension to heaven in a fiery chariot, and the apprehension he had felt upon taking up his duties alone (see 2 Kings 2). He remembered the time when the Syrian armies had surrounded him at Dothan, and how God had sent heaven's chariots to defend and protect him (see 2 Kings 6:8-23). He recalled one of the most joyful occasions of his life when he had raised a young boy back to life. The son of the Shunammite woman had died, but when Elisha had pressed his flesh against that of the lad, God's life-giving power had come flowing through him and the boy had revived. Elisha had presented him alive to his mother (2 Kings 4:18-37).

Many had been the tests and challenges during that half-century, but always Elisha had responded with faith and confidence in the God of heaven. Now the time was rapidly approaching when he would be called to face the great and final test, the test that each person must face, when we come to the end of life's journey. How would Elisha respond now?

As he sat there considering these thoughts, there was a knock at the door. Elisha's servant ushered into his bedroom a man dressed in royal garments. It was Joash, the young king of Israel, who had heard of the aging prophet's illness and had come to pay his final respects. He had also come looking for a word of encouragement and hope for his armies that had recently been decimated by the Syrian forces (see 2 Kings 13:7). The biblical description of this scene and its aftermath has three aspects that are worth highlighting.

The first part is Elisha's mortality, the fact that he was subject to death. Second Kings 13:14 states, "Now Elisha was suffering from the illness from which he died" (NIV). We don't know exactly what this illness was. *Prophets and Kings* calls it "a lingering illness" (263). Could it have been cancer? Whatever it was, I'm not so sure it was easy for Elisha to accept the fact that his condition was fatal. Now you might ask, "Why not? Why couldn't he accept it? It wasn't unusual for an old man to get seriously ill. After all, everyone died of something or other." Well, not quite everyone. As noted above, his predecessor, his mentor, the man who had trained him as a prophet, Elijah, when his ministry had drawn to an end, had not died but had been whisked to heaven in a fiery chariot.

I believe that Elisha had hoped and prayed that God would send His chariot once again to take him home. It only seemed fair. Elisha had been just as faithful, had ministered with a double portion of Elijah's spirit

(2 Kings 2:9-12), and had actually performed a greater number of miracles (a Jewish tradition says he performed sixteen to Elijah's eight but it depends on which feats are counted as miracles). But as time dragged on and Elisha grew weaker and weaker, as he suffered more and more, he gained an appreciation for the truth Paul would articulate many years later when he prayed unsuccessfully for the removal of his thorn in the flesh. Not all prayers are answered in the way we would like. Sometimes God simply says, " 'My grace is sufficient for you' " (2 Corinthians 12:9).

Just as it was not easy for Elisha to accept the fact that he was going to die, it isn't easy for contemporary Christians to face their mortality. It's not an easy thing for us to think about. This is especially true for Seventh-day Adventists. We have proclaimed for so long that Jesus is coming soon, we have hoped and believed that He would return before we die.

But it behooves us to remember these five words from Hebrews 9:27: "Man is destined to die" (NIV). Human beings are mortal. We are subject to death; we do come to the end of life's journey. Even the atheists and agnostics cannot deny the validity of the Bible on this point. The righteous and the wicked, the children of God and the rebellious, are alike subject to mortality.

Psalm 103:15, 16 states it like this: "As for man, his days are like grass, he flourishes like a flower of the field; the wind blows over it and it is gone, and its place remembers it no more."

My wife occasionally plants some flowers in a planter outside our house. I'm glad she takes care of this, for in our family she is the only one with green thumbs. Whenever I take care of a plant, it has a tendency to wither and die. And while those flowers are in bloom, they are beautiful and glorious. They brighten up the whole area. But the sad part is, the blossoms only last a couple of weeks, and then the petals are fading and falling off. Yes, as the psalmist indicates, the flowers don't last forever, and neither do we.

By pointing this out, the Bible suggests to us that we had better spend some time thinking of our mortality, of the fact that we will die.

It is not saying to brood on it or become preoccupied with it or worry about it, but at least consider it. It is a tragic thing that many people give no thought to preparing for death other than purchasing a cemetery plot and choosing a gravestone. In other words, they give no thought to being ready for eternity.

An old Christian fisherman was talking one day with a young lad who came down to watch him working at the wharf. The boy was full of ambitious plans for his life, but sadly, God did not have a part in these plans. The fisherman, trying to make conversation, began quizzing the boy. "What do you plan to do with your life?" he inquired.

The boy answered, "Well, first I plan to finish school."

"And then?" the old man continued.

"I'll work for a while, make some money, and save some of my earnings," the lad replied.

"And then?"

"Well, then I'll start my own business and make even more money."

"And then?"

"Well, as soon as I have saved enough money to retire comfortably, I'll do so," the boy added.

"And then what will you do?" persisted the old man.

"I guess eventually I'll grow old and die," said the lad.

"And then what will you do?" came the pointed question. The answer was a painful silence, for to that question the boy had no answer.

As we realize that we are all approaching the end of life's journey, it is important for us to follow the counsel found in Psalm 90:12: "Teach us to number our days aright, that we may gain a heart of wisdom" (NIV). We might paraphrase this, "Our days are short, so teach us to use each day as wisely as we should."

A certain general was speaking to his troops just before the battle was to begin. The enemy army was larger than his own. It was approaching rapidly, and ammunition was running low, so the general's remarks were brief. "Men," he said, "we only have a few bullets left, so make each one count."

What the general said has an application to every one of God's children. We only have a few days left, so let's make each one count." Let's use each one wisely. Learning about our precious Savior, enjoying the love and fellowship of family and friends, remembering that our time on this earth is relatively short and brief.

Yes, as was Elisha, we are all mortal. So the question is not whether we will come to the end of life's journey, but when we come to the end, how will we respond?

To see how Elisha responded, we now turn to a second aspect from the closing scene of Elisha's life. It can be called Elisha's confidence. Second Kings 13:14-17 describes a somewhat puzzling incident. "Jehoash king of Israel went down to see him [Elisha] and wept over him. 'My father! My father!' he cried. 'The chariots and horsemen of Israel.' Elisha said, 'Get a bow and some arrows,' and he did so. 'Take the bow in your hands,' he said to the king of Israel. When he had taken it, Elisha put his hands on the king's hands. 'Open the east window,' he said, and he opened it. 'Shoot!' Elisha said, and he shot. 'The Lord's arrow of victory, the arrow of victory over Aram!' Elisha declared. 'You will completely destroy the Arameans at Aphek' "(NIV).

It is fascinating that the young king with so many years ahead of him, who had power and prestige and everything the world offers, was worried and anxious, but the man of God, who was quickly approaching death, was calm and relaxed. From a human standpoint it seems as though their roles should be reversed, but those who are Christians can understand Elisha's confidence. He was confident in God's abiding presence, and that God was still with him in his illness, that he was not alone as he languished on his bed of sickness.

He tried to encourage Joash that God would be with him also. By placing his hands over the king's hands when the king prepared to shoot the bow, Elisha was assuring him of God's ongoing presence in his life. Elisha understood what each person needs to know when they come to the end of life's journey: God is not only with us in life, He is also with us in death.

One of the most beautiful chapters of the entire Bible is Romans 8. Toward the end of this chapter, Paul asks a vital question: "Who will separate us from the love of Christ?" (Romans 8:35). Can anyone? Can anything?

He then proceeds to answer: "For I am convinced that neither death nor life, neither angels nor demons, neither the present nor the future, nor any powers, neither height nor depth, nor anything else in all creation, will be able to separate us from the love of God that is in Christ Jesus our Lord" (Romans 8:38, 39, NIV).

The date was March 2, 1791. The greatest minister in the history of England was just about to die. Shortly before his last breath, John Wesley opened his eyes, and in that strong, clear voice that was his trademark proclaimed from his deathbed, "The best of all is God is with us."

As they faced the end of life's journey, Elisha, Paul, and John Wesley were all confident in the abiding presence of God, and we should be also. Yes, we can know the truth expressed so well in the words of the old song, "I don't have to cross Jordan alone."

Not only was Elisha confident in the abiding presence of God, he was also confident in God's ultimate victory. Now the truth is, the picture was not a rosy one at the moment. The Israelite forces had only ten chariots left (see 2 Kings 13:7), but when that arrow flew out the window, Elisha proclaimed, "The Lord's arrow of victory." Elisha realized that even though he was soon to die and God's children were pressed on every side, when all was said and done, God would win the victory.

We need that confidence also. We don't know whether we will live until Jesus comes. The truth is, some Christians will while others will fall asleep and await Him in the grave. But if we are in the latter category, we can die with this confidence: God will be triumphant. Victory is certain. That is one of the major themes of the book of Revelation. It emphasizes that although the forces of wickedness have their day in the sun, although for a while they seem to flourish and prosper, although the devil comes down with great wrath, although evil is on the march, when all is said and done, God steps in, the gospel is preached round the globe, and this world ends with a complete and glorious victory for the people of God. Yes, we can be confident in the ultimate victory of God.

However, this peace and confidence is not enjoyed by everyone. The Bible makes this clear. "The wicked are like the tossing sea, which cannot rest, whose waves cast up mire and mud. 'There is no peace,' says my God, 'for the wicked' " (Isaiah 57:20, 21, NIV). By contrast, God's children can have His confidence and peace in their hearts whether they are in their twenties or in their eighties, whether death seems far away or very near.

There is a third aspect of 2 Kings 13 to highlight. We might call it "Elisha's Postscript" or "The Final Word." Second Kings 13:20 simply states, "Elisha died and was buried." Now that sounds pretty final, but the truth of the matter is, it isn't the end of the story with Elisha. His story does not end with his burial. In fact, the story of God's children never ends with their burial.

As the Bible describes it, some time later a group of Israelites were preparing to bury one of their friends when they spotted a band of Moabite raiders. Not having the time to conduct a proper funeral without endangering their own lives, they hastily tossed the corpse in Elisha's tomb. "When the body touched Elisha's bones, the man came to life and stood up on his feet" (2 Kings 13:21). Can you imagine the surprise of these men when they heard a voice behind them calling, "Wait for me!" and then looked back and saw their friend? They probably ran faster than ever.

Although there is humor in this incident, it is placed in Scripture for a purpose. It shows that God had not forgotten his prophet. God's angels were guarding that tomb. The very atmosphere of that tomb pulsated with life. The last thing, the very last thing we see in connection with the story of Elisha in Kings is not a story of death but a story of life.

It is fitting that this happened, for what happened to that dead man who was revived is a symbol of what will one day happen to Elisha himself when the Lord descends from heaven with a shout, with the voice of the archangel, and the trump of God, and the dead in Christ shall rise first (see 1 Thessalonians 4:13-17). Yes, Elisha will be raised.

Sometimes even Christians tend to forget this point, that death is not the end of the story for the children of God. It is possible that back in Elisha's day everyone knew where his tomb was located. Perhaps they had even made some nice carvings on the entrance and overlaid it with ivory. Maybe someone offered guided tours with the tour guide pointing out the tomb with the words, "Now that is the final resting place of the prophet Elisha." But that would not be true, for God's servants never go to their final resting place.

On one occasion when my wife's grandfather, Pastor H.M.S. Richards, Sr. was preaching at the Florida camp meeting, he remarked, "If you ever read in the *Adventist Review* that H. M. S. Richards has gone to his final resting place, don't believe a word of it. I'll just be taking a nap until Jesus comes."

If Elisha were writing this chapter, he would emphasize this point in conjunction with his postscript: The life of God's children has no end. Oh, yes, they do reach the end of their earthly lives. They are mortal. They die. They rest. But one day He will call them to life again. God has a glorious future for all His children in that land where there will be no sadness, no sorrow, no aging, no hospitals, no nursing homes, no cancer, and no death. May that day be soon!

CHAPTER 12

It's Time for Revival

2 Kings 22; 23; 2 Chronicles 34; 35

It was during the early part of the fifteenth century. The French and British had been fighting for nearly a century, engaged in what later became known as the Hundred Years' War. Parts of France were occupied by British soldiers, including the important city of Reims. The occupation of Reims was important because the French kings had been crowned there for the last thousand years, and British control of it had kept the crown prince from officially becoming the king. Charles VII was known as the Dauphin, but he had not been crowned since it could not be done at Reims.

This was all about to change because of a charismatic teenager. In addition to learning to cook and sew, young Joan of Arc claimed to have received heavenly visions, including one in which she said she was instructed to help free the city of Reims so the coronation could take place. Disguising herself as a boy, she journeyed to the Dauphin on horseback. Though he and his advisors were skeptical of her claims, his soldiers were encouraged by her presence. Her courage and commitment helped the French soldiers win strategic victories at Orleans and Reims, enabling Charles VII to have a coronation on July 17, 1429. While he was crowned, the so-called "Maid of France" stood by, holding a special banner.

Her military adventures were short-lived, since she was captured the following year, convicted on charges of witchcraft and heresy, and later burned to death (in the twentieth century she was canonized as a saint by the Catholic Church). However, this young woman would forever be remembered as one of the most intriguing and enigmatic figures of Europe's ongoing wars. Though on the world stage for a brief time, she changed the course of history.

In the latter part of the seventh century B.C. a young prince named Josiah became king of the Southern Kingdom of Judah. Though only a boy of eight, he exerted an important influence on events in his kingdom, particularly through his leadership in spiritual revival and reformation. Though his reign ended tragically and prematurely (see 2 Chronicles 35:20-24), prompting a lament from the prophet Jeremiah (see 2 Chronicles 35:25), the revival that took place under his rule would forever be remembered as one of the high-water marks of spiritual commitment during the entire period of the monarchy. According to Scripture, "Before him there was no king like him, who turned to the Lord with all his heart, with all his soul, and with all his might, according to all the law of Moses; nor did any like him arise after him" (2 Kings 23:25).

Since the name Josiah is synonymous with spiritual revival, it is fitting to raise the following questions when studying the biblical record of his reign: What can we learn about spiritual revival from the time of Josiah? What were the key features and characteristics of the revival under Josiah, and what application or relevance do they have today?

Before turning to these questions, perhaps we should briefly consider an even more foundational question. What does the word *revival* mean? What is a spiritual revival? Since "to revive" means "to bring back to life," spiritual revival is the renewal of spiritual life. It connotes a renewed focus on spiritual things, a renewed commitment to the Lord, a renewed walk with the Lord Jesus Christ. In the words of Ellen White, "Revival signifies a renewal of spiritual life, a quickening of the powers of mind and heart, a resurrection from spiritual death" (*Selected Messages,* 1:128).

With this definition in mind, let us turn to what we can learn about spiritual revival from the reign of Josiah. The first point worth noting is a basic presupposition Josiah and those who assisted him must have held. As they viewed the spiritual condition of the people, as they engaged in a spiritual diagnosis, they knew that the people of God were in need of revival.

There were many signs of this need for revival. Idolatrous images and pagan altars littered the landscape (see 2 Chronicles 34:3-7). The knowledge of God's written Word had been lost (see 2 Chronicles 34:14-21). The entire community of faith had not come together to celebrate the festival of the Passover for many years (see 2 Chronicles 35:18). Spiritually speaking, the people of Judah hardly had a pulse. They were on spiritual life-support, desperately in need of revival.

Are God's people any different today? Are we any more alive spiritually than were the people of ancient Judah? We may claim to be, but several things indicate otherwise. Our preoccupation with material things, the way we spend our time, our entertainment practices, our spiritual lethargy and apathy, all testify to our need for revival.

The Divine Physician diagnoses our true condition: " 'I know your works; you have a name of being alive, but you are dead' " (Revelation 3:1). A second diagnosis confirms this previous one: "A revival of true godliness among us is the greatest and most urgent of all our needs. To seek this should be our first work" (*Selected Messages,* 1:121). You might as well stop reading this chapter right here unless you agree with this foundational point: God's people are in need of revival. We need to be spiritually revived, to be spiritually energized, to receive a new focus and new priorities in our lives. Unless we recognize this need, nothing will happen.

A second point to note from Josiah's revival is that revival begins in the heart of a single individual. Allow me to back up for a moment and rephrase that. I should say it this way: Humanly speaking, revival begins in the heart of a single individual. For in actuality, revival begins with the work of God on an individual's heart. As 1 John 4:19 implies

("We love because He first loved us."), when we reach out in love to God it is because His love has already been reaching out to us.

Theologians have a fancy term they use, which is "prevenient grace." While it is not important that Christians be able to pronounce the term and incorporate it in their working vocabularies, it is important to understand the concept. Whenever we turn toward God, it is merely a response, for His grace has already been working in our hearts. He takes the initiative.

But back to my main point. From a human standpoint, revival begins in the heart of a single individual. According to the Bible, "Josiah was eight years old when he began to reign; he reigned thirty-one years in Jerusalem. He did what was right in the sight of the Lord, and walked in the ways of his ancestor David; he did not turn aside to the right or to the left" (2 Chronicles 34:1-2). Although he was just a lad of eight, although idolatrous influences pervaded his kingdom, although his task must have seemed daunting and enormous, he sensed that God wanted him to light the spark of spiritual revival in the kingdom of Judah. He felt that one person could make a difference.

History is replete with numerous examples demonstrating the truth of this principle. A recent book entitled *Heroes of the Cold War* documented the influence certain key individuals had on the outcome of the twentieth century and the positive difference they made. One of the key points of the book is that a single person can make a huge difference. Positive events and outcomes are not inevitable, as they are sometimes held to be. Rather, positive results are achieved because of the commitment of key individuals to make a positive difference in the world.

This same point is demonstrated in medicine, science, and many other fields. Most any great discovery or invention or progress began in the heart of a single individual. It is true in spiritual matters as well. A certain man of Tarsus felt driven to take the gospel to the Gentile world. A German monk named Martin Luther felt compelled to share the truth of righteousness by faith. An English preacher named John Wesley sensed the need to proclaim the importance of living a holy and committed life. And long ago, a young king named Josiah felt called to bring spiritual revival to his people.

And what of you and me? Do we understand the significance of the truth that revival begins in the heart of one person? Are we willing to act on that truth? Not that the revival ends with one person, because once the revival begins, once the train is leaving the station, others feel moved to hop aboard. However, just as every great fire begins with a single spark or a single match, so every great revival begins in the heart of one person. Might that person be you?

A third point that emerges from the revival under Josiah is that revival occurs when people truly seek the Lord. Speaking of Josiah, Scripture declares, "For in the eighth year of his reign, while he was still a boy, he began to seek the God of his ancestor David" (2 Chronicles 34:3).

The word *seek* is a key word in this section of Scripture. According to the Lord, it is when His people seek Him and turn from their wicked ways that He is able to forgive them (see 2 Chronicles 7:14). Some other kings, such as Jehoshaphat (see 2 Chronicles 19:3) and Uzziah (see 2 Chronicles 26:5) sought the Lord, but none did it to the extent of Josiah. The driving ambition of his life, his passion, was to know God better and to follow Him "with all his heart, with all his soul, and with all his might" (2 Kings 23:25). This is what it means to seek God.

Perhaps it is uncomfortable to answer, but the question must be asked: Do we really seek God today? Oh, yes, we may go to church and even drop some money in the offering plate, but is God truly our focus in life?

The Lord declared through the prophet Jeremiah: "When you search for me, you will find me; if you seek me with all your heart" (Jeremiah 29:13). If truth were told, there is too much feeble seeking of the Lord going on, too much shallow seeking of Him. When we want to know the Lord as badly as we want air after being underwater for several minutes, when we desire God as much as we desire water when we are parched and dry on a scorching hot day, then we know what it means to seek God with all our heart. The psalmist said, "As a deer longs for flowing streams, so my soul longs for you, O God. My soul thirsts for God, for the living God" (Psalm 42:1, 2). When we desire God that much, when we really yearn to know Him better with every fiber of our being, revival takes place.

Another point worth noting from Josiah's revival is that revival involves eliminating things that impede our spiritual commitment. Just as Josiah purged the land of idols, so for us revival involves getting rid of things that hinder us in our walk with God.

Actually, a word related to revival should be mentioned at this point, namely, reformation. God wants both to take place. We have defined revival as a renewal of spiritual life. Reformation is related but distinct. It signifies change, "change in ideas and theories, habits and practices" (*Selected Messages,* 1:128). It calls for a removal of whatever might be holding us back from walking more closely with Jesus.

Reform is needed in conjunction with revival. It was true in Gideon's day when he was called to pull down his father's altar to Baal (see Judges 6:25-27). It was true in King Asa's day when he had to remove his own mother from her post as queen mother because of her idolatrous worship (see 1 Kings 15:13). It was true for Josiah when he found it necessary to destroy numerous idolatrous shrines in the land (see 2 Chronicles 34:3-7).

What changes might be needed in our lives? In what areas are reform needed? What do we need to give up?

Several years back I went to run in a road race. The distance was ten kilometers (6.2 miles). I noticed that prior to the race some people were walking around with weight belts on. The idea behind a weight belt is this: Someone who stretches, does warm-ups, and jogs around a bit prior to the race with an extra ten pounds on will feel lighter and faster once they remove the weight belt. You can be sure of this, though: Once the race began, every runner had their weight belt off.

If we are to be truly alive in Christ, if we are to experience the spiritual growth that we desire, the Bible calls us to "lay aside every weight and the sin that clings so closely, and let us run with perseverance the race that is set before us, looking to Jesus" (Hebrews 12:1, 2). Revival involves reformation. It involves change, and it means getting rid of those things that hold us back in our walk with the Lord.

An additional point that should be made from studying the revival in Josiah's day is that revival is based on the written Word of God. It is not simply based on someone's whim or notion of how God should be worshiped and served. There is an integral connection with revival and God's Word.

In the time of Josiah a key event helped further the revival. In the eighteenth year of his reign (622 B.C.), "the priest Hilkiah found the book of the law of the Lord given through Moses" (2 Chronicles 34:14). The fact that this law book—probably the book of Deuteronomy or some portion of it—had been lost is probably a sad commentary on the state of religious affairs during the reign of Manasseh, Josiah's grandfather.

When this book was read to the king, it produced a dramatic effect: "When the king heard the words of the law, he tore his clothes" (2 Chronicles 34:19). The book of the law exposed the failings of the people and revealed how far they were from God, and Josiah sensed their danger. But instead of giving up in despair, the king determined "to follow the Lord, keeping his commandments, his decrees, and his statutes, with all his heart and all his soul, to perform the words of the covenant that were written in this book" (2 Chronicles 34:31). Instead of burning the scroll like his son Jehoiakim would later do when indicted by God's Word (see Jeremiah 36:20-24), he chose to reform his ways and do all he could to bring his life into harmony with God's instructions.

The proclamation and study of the Word of God have played a major role in bringing about revival down through history. Whether during Nehemiah's time (see Nehemiah 8:1-13), during the Protestant Reformation, or during the early days of the Advent movement, true revival has always been propelled by God's Word. In fact, the Bible

113

tends to safeguard revivals, keeping them from turning aside into fanatical observances or excessive emotional display.

God wants to revive His people again today. For this to happen, we must make a renewed commitment to the study and understanding of the Bible. We must put behind us the days in which we take no time to feast on the Word of God. We must remember the truth that "one does not live by bread alone, but by every word that comes from the mouth of the Lord" (Deuteronomy 8:3)—a verse that was probably in the portion of Scripture found in Josiah's time.

It is true that we are busy. We cram our schedules with too many activities. But if we can find time to partake of physical food a few times a day, surely we can find time to feast on the Word of God. The spark of revival is lit and fanned into flame when we take time to study God's holy Word.

Another point that emerges from the biblical story of Josiah's revival is that revival needs to include the entire community of faith. While as noted above, revival may start in the heart of a single individual, if it is to be sustained, if it is to really accomplish what God wants it to, it must involve all of the people of God.

Certainly Josiah recognized this. After hearing the words from the law book read to him, he invited the leaders of the people for a covenant renewal service in which he joined them in pledging faithfulness to the Word of God (see 2 Chronicles 34:29-32). Moreover, he led out in the celebration of the Passover feast. So joyful and enriching was the occasion that "no Passover like it had been kept in Israel since the days of the prophet Samuel; none of the kings of Israel had kept such a Passover as was kept by Josiah" (2 Chronicles 35:18). Revival and reformation were sweeping over the whole community of faith.

We have a difficult time comprehending this in Western countries. Because of a rampant—and sometimes unhealthy—individualism, we tend to see our relationship with God in individual terms. While it is true that each person is called to know God individually, it is also the case that the Bible has a strong emphasis on the community of faith. Just as one glowing ember, if isolated from the wood, will burn itself out and be unable to keep the fire going, so one isolated Christian will not be able to prompt and sustain the type of revival that God wants to take place.

The prophet Joel's understanding of revival and renewal is apropos today. All the people, including the aged and the young (see Joel 2:16) are called to be part of what God wants to do in the lives of His people. The Lord wants to do a work in each heart. Let us ensure that each person receives the invitation to be a part of what God wishes to do.

However, despite the positive lessons we can learn about revival from godly Josiah, the sad truth is that the fires of revival went out. In a little over two decades after this revival began, Josiah was tragically slain in 609 B.C. while attempting to do battle with Pharaoh Neco (see 2 Chronicles 35:20-24). And about twenty-three more years later, Jerusalem and its magnificent temple lay in smoldering ruins, having been destroyed by the Babylonian army. What happened? How did what had started so well come undone?

While we do not know all the answers to this question, one possible answer is that Josiah's revival never really took root in the hearts of his people. It may have been only skin-deep. Perhaps it involved changes in some of their practices and external observances, but it never really changed the heart. Jeremiah, the prophetic contemporary of Josiah, called on the people to "circumcise yourselves to the Lord, remove the foreskins of your hearts" (Jeremiah 4:4). If change is only external, it is not of lasting value. True revival calls upon God's people as follows: "Yet even now, says the Lord, return to me with all your heart, with fasting, with weeping, and with mourning; rend your hearts and not your clothing" (Joel 2:12, 13).

Before this chapter concludes, I wish to raise two questions, not about Josiah's revival of long ago, but about the revival that God wants to take place today. The first question is this: Will you and I be a part of this revival? Or will we sit on the sidelines, finding fault with some aspect of what God is doing or complaining about some perceived slight or mistreatment?

Revival will take place, or better yet, it is taking place! God has promised, "I will pour out my spirit on all flesh" (Joel 2:28), and this is going on in our day. There is a danger of having the latter rain of God's Spirit falling all around us while we are oblivious to it all. Will we invite the Spirit to do a work of revival in our lives?

The second question is simply this: If I invite the Lord to do a work of revival in me, will it make a lasting difference in my life? Will it be a revival focused only on externals, only skin-deep, or will it penetrate to the core of my being, to my very heart?

You see, the ultimate question for me is not what happened to the revival in Josiah's day, but will I allow God to revive my heart today?

CHAPTER 13

Light at the End of the Tunnel

2 Kings 24; 25; 2 Chronicles 36; Jeremiah 31:31-34; Ezekiel 36:22-32

He sat in my office and poured out his aching heart to me. Tears came to his eyes as he spoke of his deep anguish over the fact that his girlfriend had broken up with him. He recounted the history of their dating relationship. He told me how they had first started dating and about the good times they had had. He shared the details of the painful day when he had learned that she no longer wanted a special relationship with him. He related some of his clumsy and ultimately fruitless attempts to win back her affection. He had invested loads of time and lots of money in his relationship with her, and he could not bear to see it come to an end. He was hurting so badly that it seemed as if his heart would break.

As he cried in my office that day, he felt dejected and downcast. He was locked in despair. He wondered why this had to happen to him. He pondered whether there was any reason for him to have hope in the future. Could he ever be happy again? Why was it worthwhile to keep on going without her as his girlfriend? What was there to give him some light at the end of the tunnel?

Over two-and-a-half millennia ago, God's covenant people came up hard against some of these same questions. Both 2 Kings 25 and 2 Chronicles 36 describe the terrible tragedy that had occurred to them at the hands of Nebuchadnezzar and the Babylonian army. Their houses had been razed and burned. The walls of the city of Jerusalem had been demolished. The magnificent temple, the house of the Lord Himself, the splendid structure which was the pride of the nation, lay in charred ruins. Most of the people that had not been killed had been carried away into exile in a hostile nation. Those who remained behind in the land looked at a very uncertain future.

Both the exiles and those remaining in the land faced a terrible crisis of confidence. Questions abounded, and answers were few. Why had all these things happened to them? Where was God in all of this? Had He abandoned them? What was there to give them hope for the future? What was there to give light at the end of the tunnel?

Scripture provides some answers in response to these issues, and in the rest of this chapter, I would like to explore the biblical response to two different questions: First, why had this disaster occurred? If a repeat of this ancient disaster is to be avoided, it is important to understand why it took place. And second, what was there to give them hope for the future? God's contemporary children will sometimes face seemingly hopeless situations, as His people did in biblical times. We will sometimes be locked in depression and despair. When we are in these times, it will be helpful to understand what gave them hope to keep on going in their darkest night.

Though the answer to the first question is multifaceted, there is one point the Bible clearly makes. Not just once but repeatedly. One of the main reasons why Jerusalem fell and the people were taken off into exile was the people's unwillingness to listen to God's warnings through His prophets.

The Bible puts it this way: "The Lord, the God of their ancestors, sent persistently to them by his messengers, because he had compassion on his people and on his dwelling place; but they kept mocking the messengers of God, despising his words, and scoffing at his prophets, until the wrath of the Lord against his people became so great that there was no remedy" (2 Chronicles 36:15, 16).

God really did try to warn His people. He spoke to them again and again, warning them of the ruin and disaster to which their sin would lead. But they refused to listen. Unfortunately, the message declared by King Jehoshaphat had never taken root. When confronted with an invasion, he had stood up and proclaimed, " 'Listen to me, O Judah and inhabitants of Jerusalem! Believe in the Lord your God and you will be established; believe his prophets' " (2 Chronicles 20:20).

Reflection on these powerful and profound verses raises the same issue for God's children today: Do we do any better at listening to the messengers of God than the ancient inhabitants of Jerusalem? Do we follow their counsel today? Are we willing to have our lives shaped and molded by what God's prophets—whether ancient or modern—proclaim? Or when we come across some area where our lives stand in opposition to a message from a prophet, is it easier to dismiss the prophet as being unacquainted with the complexities of modern life?

If the answer offered above as to the reason for their disaster is correct, it is also correct to say that the people's own choices led to the tragedy that befell them. In other words, it was their own fault. They could not legitimately blame their dismal situation on God or on the Babylonians or on their ancestors, as they were sometimes prone to do (see Ezekiel 18:2). The face that caused all their problems was the face in the mirror.

It is important to be aware of this when we are confronted with difficulties today. In the church the main problems that we face are not the ones brought about by external forces. Rather, as someone stated it, "We have met the enemy, and it is us." The main challenges that we have, the chief problems that arise, are the ones that come from within. That is to say, our own choices and actions are usually responsible for the problems we face.

Another point worth noting at this juncture is that when God's people slight and ignore His messengers and violate His principles, it is to their own detriment. It has a boomerang effect, resulting in harm to themselves. Jesus said, " 'I came that they may have life, and have it abundantly' " (John 10:10). Jesus truly desires for His people to experience a life that is fulfilled and blessed in notable ways, but for that to happen, we need to follow His principles. When we turn our backs on His instruction, it is bound to cause us difficulty.

Several months ago my family was at a retreat held at the biological field station run by Pacific Union College on the California coast. One afternoon my wife noticed that our youngest son Joshua was flirting with danger by sitting on a high handrail, dangling his legs in the air. Worried about a potential injury, she told him to keep his feet on the ground and to stay off the handrail. Later that same day, someone at the retreat came to my wife and said, "You need to come. Your son has been in an accident." Sure enough, he had fallen off the handrail and slammed his head hard on the concrete, opening a deep gash. We hopped in our van and raced for the hospital. The doctor eventually told us he was going to be OK, but the diagnosis and treatment included a painful shot, stitches, an MRI, and a missed evening of fun at the retreat. All because he had refused to heed the warning.

Often, like ancient Israel and like my son at this retreat, we ignore the warnings to us and we slight instruction. It only leads to pain; it results in our own hurt. If we really want to experience and enjoy the abundant life God wants us to have, the best way is to follow His principles and obey His Word.

We come now to the second question raised above. It was a crucial question if God's ancient people were to have a positive attitude toward the future, if they were to find any glimmers of light in the midst of their misery and despair. The question is this: What was there to give them hope for the future? On what was their hope to be based? What was the light at the end of the tunnel that must have seemed so long and dark to them?

The Bible answers this question in a couple of ways. The first one worth noting is the simple truth that God hadn't given up on His people. He still had a plan for them. The final chapter in their story was yet to be written. In fact, we might say that God's love never gives up on His people, sinful and wicked though they be. His love, mercy, and kindness come from an inexhaustible source and are never depleted.

The prophet Isaiah declared, "For the mountains may depart and the hills be removed, but my steadfast love shall not depart from you, and my covenant of peace shall not be removed, says the Lord who has compassion on you" (Isaiah 54:10). Do we really grasp the significance of this verse? Even if the tallest mountains, some of our most permanent and enduring landmarks around, should disappear, God's love never will.

On the whole, the book of Lamentations describes a grim and dismal situation. It was a dirge, a funeral poem, composed on the occasion of the siege and destruction of the city of Jerusalem. But right near the middle of the five chapters of this doleful book, the bright light of hope flashes. We read, "But this I call to mind, and therefore I have hope: The steadfast love of the Lord never ceases, his mercies never come to an end; they are new every morning; great is your faithfulness" (Lamentations 3:21-23).

When we face difficulties today, when our own spiritual lives are not what they should be, or when our children rebel against every value and principle we have attempted to pass along to them, this fact should give us hope: God's love never comes to an end. His mercies are new every day.

The biblical books of Kings and Chronicles have a fascinating strategy of highlighting the truth that God hadn't given up on His covenant people. It is instructive to note how both books end. Right at the conclusion of 2 Kings, after the description of Jerusalem's destruction, we find what seems like, at first glance, a strange passage. "In the thirty-seventh year of the exile of King Jehoiachin of Judah, in the twelfth month, on the twenty-seventh day of the month, King Evil-merodach of Babylon, in the year that he began to reign, released King Jehoiachin of Judah from prison; he spoke kindly to him, and gave him a seat above the other seats of the kings who were with him in Babylon. So Jehoiachin put aside his prison clothes. Every day of his life he dined regularly in the king's presence. For his allowance, a regular allowance was given him by the king, a portion every day, as long as he lived" (2 Kings 25:27-30).

This mention of Jehoiachin's being released and allowed to eat at the king's table after thirty-seven years of imprisonment sounds a note of hope at the end of a bleak performance. It is meant to underscore the following truth: God is working redemptively on behalf of His people. He hasn't given up on them, even though many of them are in exile. There is a star in the darkest night. Similarly, right at the end of 2 Chronicles, the Bible highlights Cyrus's release of the captives who would rebuild the temple of the Lord, again showing the sunshine of God's love breaking through the clouds of exile.

I read somewhere that the Mississippi River, America's most famous river, discharges an average of 640,000 cubic feet of water *per second* into the Gulf of Mexico. This is an incredible amount of water! Someone might think that with this volume of water the so-called "father of waters" might finally run dry, that its source up in Lake Itasca, Minnesota might be depleted. But it doesn't happen. The water keeps right on flowing, day after day, month after month, year after year.

The Mississippi River is a fitting symbol of God's love and mercy, for they keep right on flowing. They are never depleted or exhausted. This truth should provide hope and comfort for us whenever we are in what is sometimes called the "dark night of the soul." God's love never gives up on His people. His mercy never comes to an end. It is new every morning.

One way that we know that God hadn't given up on His people is that He was constantly inviting them to return to Him. The prophet Jeremiah, who prophesied during the last days of the history of the kingdom of Judah, repeatedly issued the invitation. He called, "Return, faithless Israel" (Jeremiah 3:12), and "Return, O faithless children" (Jeremiah 3:14; see also Jeremiah 3:22). It seems that one of the Lord's favorite words is "Return," the word of invitation.

Several things are implicit in God's invitation to His people to come back to Him. First, the fact that they have strayed away. As Isaiah states, "All we like sheep have gone astray" (Isaiah 53:6). Second, the fact that God wants them back. And finally, it indicates that He will accept them if they do come back to Him.

A second way that the Bible answers the question of what could give the people of God hope amidst their bleak circumstances is through the magnificent promises found in the prophetic books. These books, written to provide hope and comfort for the covenant people during the very dark days of impending destruction and exile, contain some of the most thrilling promises in all of Scripture. Some of these promises are contained in the passages where Jeremiah and Ezekiel describe God's plan for a new covenant with His people (see Jeremiah 31:31-34 and Ezekiel 36:22-32).

Several of these promises are worth highlighting. One of the foremost is God's promise to forgive the sins of His people. In Jeremiah's classic description of the new covenant, the Lord declares, "I will forgive their iniquity, and remember their sin no more" (Jeremiah 31:34).

Because some of us have heard God's promise of forgiveness all of our lives, we tend to take it for granted. The true significance of it has been lost. Perhaps God's ancient people were the same. But its importance and value should not be lost. God was saying that He was willing to cleanse His people from all their sins, no matter what they had done.

And to demonstrate that His words were no empty promise, God had already demonstrated the depth and breadth of His forgiveness with

Manasseh, Judah's most wicked king. Notwithstanding Manasseh's rampant idolatry and child sacrifice performed upon his own son (see 2 Chronicles 33:1-11), when Manasseh humbled himself and turned to God, "God received his entreaty, heard his plea, and restored him again to Jerusalem and to his kingdom" (2 Chronicles 33:13).

The Lord's willingness to forgive gave hope to Manasseh, it provided hope for the rest of the people of God, and it should give hope to us today. Often one of the main reasons for our hopelessness is the knowledge of our own mistakes. Either we have not done as we ought or we have done as we ought not—sins of omission or sins of commission. As we see the tragic results of our sins, as we see our iniquities repeated in the lives of our children, we are tempted to despair. When this happens, when the magnitude of our mistakes and sins presses down upon us, let us remember God's promise to forgive. He will wipe our slates clean. He will remember our sins no more. As *Steps to Christ* states it, "If you give yourself to Him, and accept Him as your Savior, then, sinful as your life may have been, for His sake you are accounted righteous. Christ's character stands in place of your character, and you are accepted before God just as if you had not sinned" (62).

Another promise that provided some light at the end of the tunnel for God's ancient people was His promise to them of a new heart. Speaking through Ezekiel to His exiled people, the Lord pledged, "A new heart I will give you, and a new spirit I will put within you; and I will remove from your body the heart of stone and give you a heart of flesh" (Ezekiel 36:26). The very next verse helps explain what this new heart was all about, namely, a mind that would be receptive to the prompting of the Holy spirit, a mind that would be eager to follow the will of God. "I will put my Spirit within you, and make you follow my statutes, and be careful to observe my ordinances" (Ezekiel 36:27). No longer would the people of God be unresponsive to God's warnings and impervious to His pleadings, people "who would not listen but were stubborn" (2 Kings 17:14). In other words, the gift of a new heart would lead them to follow the ways of God. It would result in a committed life.

As we consider the two promises noted above, an important point needs to be made. So many times Christians misunderstand or get off the track on the matter of the relationship between forgiveness and transformation, but the Bible speaks with clarity on this point. At the time we receive God's forgiveness, we also receive His gift of a new heart that is eager to follow God's will. When we are cleansed, we start being transformed. When we are justified or forgiven by God, our process of sanctification, our growth into His likeness, also commences. While the two events are distinct, they cannot be divorced from one another.

The book *The Desire of Ages* has a magnificent description of what happens in our lives as we receive the gift of a new heart. "If we consent, He will so identify Himself with our thoughts and aims, so blend our hearts and minds into conformity to His will, that when obeying Him we shall be but carrying out our own impulses. The will, refined and sanctified, will find its highest delight in doing His service. When we know God as it is our privilege to know Him, our life will be a life of continual obedience. Through an appreciation of the character of Christ, through communion with God, sin will become hateful to us" (668). In other words, as we receive God's gift of a new heart, it becomes natural for us to follow the divine will.

I can remember as a boy of nine years old being amazed by the electrifying news that Dr. Christiaan Barnard had performed the first heart transplant in Cape Town, South Africa. It was an astonishing thought to me at the time, that the heart of one person could actually be taken out and replaced with another person's heart and the first person still be living. But as I reflect on this decades-ago event, it strikes me that Barnard's idea was not new. God started doing heart transplants long ago. And to be precise, what God does should be called a heart "implant" instead of a heart "transplant," because it is not another sinful human heart He is giving us. Instead, His gift is a heart attuned to spiritual things, one that is eager to listen to God's voice and do His will.

Whatever darkness may be overshadowing our lives, whatever night into which we may have descended, be it our struggle with pride and selfishness or something more visible like sexual sin or self-control, God offers His new heart as a gift to us.

The final promise we will explore that provided hope for God's ancient people was the promise of a renewed relationship with Him. The Lord declared through Jeremiah, "I will be their God, and they shall be my people" (Jeremiah 31:33). Ezekiel emphasized the same point (see Ezekiel 36:28). There was light at the end of the tunnel! No longer would they be estranged from God, alienated because of their sinful choices (see Isaiah 59:2). Now they would belong to Him, they would truly be *His* people, and He would be *their* God.

This relationship would be a close, personal friendship. As Jeremiah described this relationship when he proclaimed, "They shall all know me" (Jeremiah 31:34). It is worth noting that the Hebrew word for "know" (*yada*) is the same word that is sometimes used to describe the closest human relationship possible, the union of husband and wife (see Genesis 4:1). In other words, God wanted His people then, as well as His people today, to have the closest relationship possible, a friendship with true intimacy.

How would this relationship be possible? This in itself could only come about by divine grace. "I will give them a heart to know that I am the Lord" (Jeremiah 24:7). This is part of the transformation of heart. God was the One who placed in the hearts of His Old Testament people, who places in the hearts of His children today, a desire to know Him. That is how we come to know Him personally and intimately. This desire of the heart is a gift of divine grace.

Times of darkness were not limited to ancient Israel. Long, dark tunnels occur today—times when we experience the dark night of the soul. When we look at the world, we are sometimes overwhelmed by its rampant secularism and moral relativism. When we consider the church, we are at times discouraged by its spiritual apathy and lukewarmness. And most disturbingly, when we contemplate our own lives, we see misguided priorities and a lack of spiritual commitment. With anguish in our heart we raise the question articulated by ancient Israel: What can give us hope in such times? What is the light at the end of our tunnel?

Simply this: God hasn't given up on us, for His love and mercy are never depleted. He invites us to return to Him. And He promises us His forgiveness, a new heart, and a new relationship with Him. What more do we need?

If you enjoyed this book, you'll enjoy these as well:

Knowing God in the Real World

Jon Paulien. Is the gospel still relevant in the 21st century? Paulien clarifies the basics of the gospel message, and demonstrates how that message can be expressed in a way that makes sense in the secular world.

0-8163-1812-3. Paperback. US$12.99, Cdn$20.99.

Shades of Grace

Ty Gibson. Shades of Grace is a series of penetrations into the mind and emotions of God. You will discover that His grace, far from being a sterile legal provision, is the outpouring of a divine love that will not let us go at any cost to Himself.

0-8163-1852-2. Paperback. US$12.99, Cdn$20.99.

The Gift

An unforgettable look at the sacrifice of Christ. *The Gift,* by Kim Allan Johnson, will put you back in touch with the God who would rather go to hell for you than to live in heaven without you.

0-8163-1768-2. Paperback. US$11.99, Cdn$19.49

Order from your ABC by calling **1-800-765-6955**, or get online and shop our virtual store at **www.adventistbookcenter.com**.

- Read a chapter from your favorite book
- Order online
- Sign up for email notices on new products